Finally, a Permanent Solution to Changing What is Invisibly Controlling You!

The Unconscious AUTHORITY

How to break through your mind's barriers, unleash your dormant wisdom and banish limitations in your life, relationships or career.

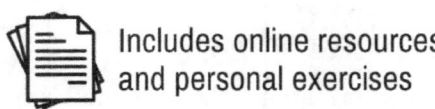

Includes online resources and personal exercises

Joe Hammer

Copyright © 2015, 2025 by Joe Hammer
All rights reserved.

Published by Forerunner Publishing
Scottsdale, Arizona | www.ForerunnerPublishing.net

Cover design by Joe Hammer, That Small Business Guy
www.ThatSmallBusinessGuy.com

Joe Hammer has asserted his right to be identified as the author of this Work in accordance with the Copyright, Designs and Patents Act 1988.

No part of this publication may be reproduced, stored in a retrieval system, or transmitted in any form or by any means, electronic, mechanical, photocopying, recording or otherwise, except as permitted under Section 107 or 108 of the 1976 United States Copyright Act, without the prior written permission of the author.

Limit of Liability/Disclaimer of Warranty: While the author and publisher have used their best effort in preparing this book, they make no representations or warranties with respect to the accuracy or completeness of the contents of this book and specifically disclaim any implied warranties of merchantability or fitness for a particular purpose. The advice contained herein may not be suitable for your situation. You should consult with a professional where appropriate. Neither the author nor publisher shall be liable for damages arising herefrom.

    ISBN-10: 0996804706
    ISBN-13: 978-0-9968047-0-7

Bound and printed and in The United States of America

To buy additional copies of this book, visit the author's website at www.UnconsciousAuthority.com, www.Amazon.com or www.IngramContent.com

For more information on Joe Hammer's speaking and coaching services, please contact him via his official web sites portal: www.JoeHammer.com

5 Star Amazon Reviews!

Very powerful life changing book. The author makes it very easy to read and understand. We all go through different stages in our life! How many times have you found yourself blindly walking in circles stock in a place or situation in life but deep inside you know you are fully capable to move on but you just can't? The Unconscious Authority not only clearly explains why, but gives you the tools to help you move to the next level and reach those desirable goals. I downloaded the exercises forms and I am in the middle of the process. I will update my review once I meet my goal. I am also listening the Ultra Depth audio suggested by the author and it has been an amazing journey so far! Thank you! It feels just amazing when one can take control of what couldn't be achieved before! Not only my life is changing but the ones around me are feeling that powerful change as well. Kids, family, co-workers and friends! I highly recommend this book to everyone! No one is perfect! We all have a past somewhere that could be blocking some areas of our present life! ...why not give this powerful book a try? In my opinion this is the type of book that should be available in other languages.

A DELIGHTFUL and insightful read, Joe Hammer has brought together the best teachings on "how the mind works", while adding his own creative genius. You will be energized and inspired! Highly recommend!

Joe Hammer gives significantly practical and easy to follow steps to approaching making changes in one's life through his innovative concept of the Unconscious Authority. The book is not only full of highly valuable resources and tools you can put into practice into your life today to make a positive change but is very enjoyable to read as well. Joe's approach addresses what many self-help/personal developments books fail to do, addressing the root causes of problem areas in our lives. Highly Recommended!

Love this book it has been a great help for me, Joe is great and very helpful, I recommend this book to anyone who wants to try it! Super happy with it.

What I liked about the book is that it explained how the conscious brain can be "tricked" by our past thoughts and experiences. We may want to change a pattern in our life but unless we change the existing "program" we will fail to get the results we are looking for. Joe Hammer explains in his own style and through his own discoveries ways to re instruct the past so we can live in the present without our old "programs" running the show.

The Unconscious Authority takes the reader on an enjoyable, easy to read journey through the inner workings of the mind. It explains why we seem to repeat old patterns or may be unable to move past inner conflict and obstacles in order to manifest our desires. The author offers guidance and downloadable worksheets that will assist the reader in developing their own clear intention for change along with a technique to bring chance to fruition. Highly recommended!

Joe Hammer has written a wonderful book filled with practical tools and applications for understanding not only where we are stuck but how to significantly change the negative habits and thoughts that have kept us there. I thoroughly enjoyed the material, humor and practical applications that Joe presents in this book. I recommend it for anyone searching for support in making significant life changes in a positive way.

I always appreciate books that invite me to think differently AND act differently!! This is one of those books. It feels like as I read the words are inviting new synopsis of my brain to fire off. This book is a great opportunity to learn and to learn to change. It is chock full of great information, examples and fun!!

Love your Book and Ultra Depth CD. Joe, we are from the same hometown and you are the best. I have been listening to your cd totally awesome. I feel so free. The book I printed off the worksheets. Doing those. So empowering. Just love you my dearest friend. I miss you so much. Can't wait for what else you have up your sleeve. May God keep blessing you.

This book is full of great information that has been studied thoroughly by Joe Hammer. A real HOW TO, that can lead to great results. This book is a wonderful tool, but it can't do the work for you, hence all the great knowledge that Joe shares must be implemented by the reader! Joe's energy is contagious and not only is the book outstanding, but Joe is a great speaker and was a wonderful guest sharing his knowledge and passion with my listeners on WKKX! Thanks, Joe, for all you do to help us all lead our best and greatest life!

WOW, what a book!! Extremely enlightening and easy to read and understand. I liked the words " Your Thoughts have power." The book is packed with suggestions, that if followed, will INDEED change your life for the better. I've known Joe for years because he live in our area. Now I have the pleasure of being neighbors with his precious Mother. Blessings and best wishes for a book that will help a lot of people.

I haven't quite finished the book yet but it's been terrific so far! The author really knows his stuff! I've read many books in this genre, but Joe offers a new twist, which peels yet another layer of the onion in terms of accessing and re-programming the mind, since he's trained in hypnosis. It's a great approach for breaking through unconscious barriers in your life. I highly recommend this book!

I urge you to read this book and follow through the step-by-step exercises. Transformation can happen. Do not take it lightly. An abundance of information... easy and fun to read. I am forever grateful to know Joe Hammer as a friend and have him as a Mentor. He is brilliant Communicator, Knowledgeable, and have a big heart for service.

As a business we are always looking for new ways to expand our services. The "Unconscious Authority" has allowed us to break through old thought patterns and discover the proverbial light at the end of the tunnel. We not only have expanded our listener base, but also found opportunities that were dormant to us. Thanks for the great book!

Reaching the ultra-depth of our unconscious mind is definitely the place to start when looking to change your life. Thanks to this book, it takes you straight there. Transformation, here I come!! Thanks again, Joe.

A rather unusual "self-help" book that presents techniques to just tweak or make over those issues that prevent success. Well written, with easy-to-understand facts and principles that can be applied right now...

I love this book. It's a short, powerful and potentially life-changing read - written in a most engaging fashion. Buy it, read it and learn how to question what you believe about yourself and discover why you behave the way you do. Next, discover an effective way to unravel the nonsense you have historically accepted as fact about yourself, and then use the techniques in the book to become the person you need to become, to do the things you need to do, to get the things you want to have. Highly recommended.

Doubt is
Fearing the Dark
Confidence is
Lighting a Candle

— Joe Hammer

Dedication

To the memory of Joseph Leonard Kessler, my "Uncle Joe."

Though not my uncle by blood, Joe was a towering figure in my life—a mentor, guide, and friend. As the heart of Kessler's Farm Fresh Market, where my mother worked, he embodied a time when independent storeowners crafted their trade with care, before factory farming changed the landscape.

An avid horse trader, Joe made a promise when my mother was pregnant with me, "Name that boy after me, and I'll give him his first pony." True to his word, he gifted me Coco, a loyal, loving pony who trailed me like a shadow. I cherished that little guy for many years.

Joe taught me to "do things right" and to stand by my word—lessons that shape me still. A war veteran, bold entrepreneur, and masterful pony trader, he was a man of wisdom and conviction. Not a day passes without gratitude for the simple yet profound life lessons he shared.

Thank you, Uncle Joe. Your legacy lives on in me.

Contents

Preface 1

A Note to the Reader 11

Introduction 15
    What is The Unconscious Authority? 15
    Your State of Being (Why Am I Like This?) 17
    External Domain vs. Internal Dominion 19
    The Creative Mind 21
    The Master Recording Device (Your Brain on Autopilot) 23
    What Would You Like To Chang In Your Life? 26
    Ink It (Seriously, Grab a Pen…) 30
    What You'll Learn 36
    Okay Little Buddy, It's Time to Get to Work 38

The Formation of Our Reality 43
    Illusions 43
    Perceptions: The Funhouse Mirrors of the Mind 45
    Beliefs: The Invisible Puppet Masters 46
    Luck? Who Says? 49
    My Bread Crust Story 54

The Habit of Thought 63
    Your Thoughts Have Power 65
    Your Thoughts and Feelings Are Designing Your Destiny 66
    The Law of Subtraction? 72
    The Mental Triad—Dream Team or Drama Squad? 74
    The Power of Your Words 76
    Words Influence Your Emotions 79
    The Double-Sided Excuse 84
    Authority Figures—Wisdom Gone Wild 86
    The Condescending Minister—Yeah, the Halo Slipped 88

We Become What We Contemplate 93
- Silent Signals..…..........95
- The Mind's Processors—Your Brain's "Odd Couple"......................98
- It's Time For You To Be Sick ....…........100
- Change The Channel ....…...................….102
- Kites and Anchors...….....104
- Cheerleaders and Coaches ....…........................…107
- Power and Will..…....109
- Harness your Imagination...…111
- Ready To Work That Brain Muscle?...112
- Divine Intelligence..….................115
- Get Uncomfortably Specific..119
- Money Mindset: Channeling Your Inner Wealthy Weirdo…….…...…119

The Technology of the Mind 123
- The Conscious Mind..…...........125
- The Subconscious Mind—The Master Archive ....….............135
- The Critical Faculty...158
- Talk Therapy Sometimes Falls Short ....…..................169
- Maxims of the Mind..…..............172

The Client Files..…... 179
- The Postmaster and the Barbie Doll.......................….................180
- The Trainer and the Nasty Stepmother ....….............185
- The Teacher Crush and Fear of Girls ....…...189
- The "Drag" and the Chronic Cough.........................….................193
- The Roofer and the After Dark Panic Attacks ....….........198
- Oh, That's Just Bethany..…200
- The Lifelong Stutterer...207
- The Trucker's Enduring Back Pain...212
- The Persistent Pimples..…217
- That's Illogical Captain...221

30 Days to the New and Improved You ....….... 225
- The Wake Up Call...…..................228
- Bad Bedtime Rituals...232
- Launch Your Subconscious Motivation Process!.........….............236

Hypnosis Myths and Misconceptions ....…..... 247

Meet The Author...….....261

Preface

I was 16 years old, armed with ambition, a stack of spiral notebooks, and the kind of confidence only a teenager with zero real-world experience can have. I wasn't just starting a business—I was launching a life empire. Or at least a mildly profitable custom painting business. But even back then, I had a gut feeling that success wasn't just about hustle—it had something to do with what was going on between my ears. I became fascinated with the idea that my thoughts were like the software running the whole operation, and if I didn't upgrade it, I'd be stuck buffering for life.

That curiosity turned into a full-blown obsession. While my classmates were cramming for math exams, I was devouring books on personal growth, business psychology, and anything that promised to decode the mysterious algorithm of success. I mean everything—from Napoleon Hill to Deepak Chopra. My goal? Figure out why some entrepreneurs are raking it in while others struggle to make a buck. However, I found it wasn't about talent. It was mindset—what I now call your "internal authority."

Fast forward to today, and that bookworm behavior never stopped. I've now got over a thousand titles in my personal library, most of which fall into the "Why am I like this?" section of the bookstore—psychology, health, spirituality, business, and a few that should probably come with a warning label like, "Side effects include sudden self-awareness and spontaneous

Joe **Hammer**

goal setting." I still invest in my mind and I encourage everyone else to do the same.

Now, here's where things take a turn for the wonderfully weird... in addition to being a business nerd and a speaker, I'm also a comedy magician and improviser. That's right—card tricks and punchlines. Sleight of hand with a side of sass. Making stuff up. I've spent years blending wonder and laughter, making people question their eyes while snorting into their drinks.

One Friday night, I got booked to open for a stage hypnotist at a local comedy club. Naturally, as someone who tricks people for a living, I was watching him with the skepticism of a TSA agent examining a suspicious carry-on.

Right away, I wasn't buying it. His volunteers? Way too eager. Way too responsive. I'm sitting there thinking, "Come on, nobody falls asleep that fast unless they're in a staff meeting or have eaten three servings of lasagna." In the magic world, we have a term for people like that: Shills. Plants. Actors "in on the act." I figured the whole thing was staged—like a reality TV show but with less drama.

I left that night 90% unimpressed and 10% curious—mostly because a little voice in my head (probably fueled by too many self-help books) whispered, "What if it's real?" That voice turned out to be a total game-changer.

I opened for him again the next evening. This time, something shifted. The volunteers he selected were different than the night before. Two of them I recognized immediately as regulars at the club—locals I'd seen time and time again in the audience. They weren't actors, and they certainly weren't part of the show. Yet, just like the night before, they followed his instructions, appeared to enter a deep trance, and performed with complete authenticity. How could that be?

After the show, my curiosity got the best of me. I approached one of the volunteers.

"Were you really hypnotized?" I asked.

"I guess so," he said with a shrug.

"What was it like?"

"I just felt really relaxed."

"Do you remember the funny stuff you did?"

"Yeah," he said, smiling. "It was fun. I enjoyed myself—and honestly, I feel great."

That brief exchange cracked something open in me. Here was a regular guy, no stage experience, no acting background, who had seemingly gone under hypnosis and loved the experience. If this was real, then I had just witnessed the power of the mind in action—live, unfiltered, and transformative.

That moment marked the beginning of a new chapter in my life. I developed a fascination with stage hypnosis. Driven by both curiosity and a hunger to understand what was really happening, I booked a flight to Las Vegas and trained with some of the

Joe **Hammer**

top professional stage hypnotists in the country. What began as skepticism turned into hands-on study. Not long after, I added a full-blown stage hypnosis show to my entertainment repertoire—one that brought together comedy, curiosity, and a healthy respect for the subconscious mind.

But something deeper was calling. During these shows, I witnessed how a simple suggestion, such as, "Your face is itchy," or "The person next to you smells horrible"... could produce a real, visceral reaction. That's when it hit me... if I could make someone believe something unpleasant through suggestion, couldn't I use the same process to help them believe something empowering? Could hypnosis be used not just for laughs, but for healing?

The answer came quickly and clearly... I needed to learn hypnotherapy—the therapeutic, transformative side of hypnosis.

I dove in. I immersed myself in the study of hypnotherapy, determined to understand how this misunderstood tool could be used to create real and lasting change. What I discovered was a modality with a rich history and an impressive track record for helping people overcome anxiety, break habits, build confidence, and shift long-standing mental patterns. Hypnotherapy wasn't just parlor tricks—it was a bridge between the conscious and subconscious mind. And when used with care and intention, it could unlock a person's greatest potential.

Today, I've integrated hypnotherapy into my speaking, mentoring, and coaching work. It has become one of the most powerful tools in my toolkit—helping people move beyond surface-level

The Unconscious **Authority**

thinking and into deeper transformation. It all began with a little skepticism, a lot of curiosity, and a willingness to be surprised by the mind's incredible ability to change itself.

However I quickly discovered something funny—and not "haha" funny, but "huh, that's odd" funny—about most traditional hypnotherapy training. A lot of it relied on what's called *direct suggestion*. That's a fancy term for the hypnotherapist becoming a kind of motivational Siri, calmly repeating things like, "You are full. You've had enough. Step away from the cheesecake." Sounds great, right? In theory, yes. In practice... maybe not.

Take this classic example... someone's overeating, and while they're in a relaxed hypnotic state, we say something like, "From now on, you'll feel completely satisfied eating only half of what's on your plate."

Sounds good, right?

Except... what if the reason they're overeating isn't physical hunger, but emotional hunger? What if they're not reaching for seconds because they're still hungry, but because their childhood cat Mittens left them with unresolved abandonment issues? (Okay, that's dramatic, but you get the idea.)

It just didn't sit right with me. It felt like putting a motivational Band-Aid over a psychological bullet wound. Like a doctor giving you a pill for a symptom without ever asking why the symptom is happening. Sure, you might feel better for a little while, but the root of the problem is still in the background, waiting to resurface.

Joe **Hammer**

I wanted to do deeper work—the kind of work where you roll up your sleeves, grab your emotional hardhat, and get ready to crawl through the psychological crawlspace of someone's past. That's when I stumbled upon *Regressive Hypnotherapy*. And let me tell you—it was love at first regression. This method allows clients to go back in time (no DeLorean required) to uncover the original sensitizing events—the "Ohhhh, so *that's* where that started" moments—buried deep in the subconscious. These events often hold the key to why we're experiencing certain challenges in our adult lives.

So, like any enthusiastic student of the mind with a passion for healing and a flair for showmanship, I dove in. I studied, trained, practiced, and soon launched a part-time hypnotherapy practice. Clients started showing up with a wild mix of issues—from self-doubt to phobias, from emotional trauma to behavioral loops they couldn't escape. Some stories were touching, some were bizarre, and a few were so powerful they left me speechless (which, for me, is a rare and unnatural condition). Many of these stories were so impactful that they found their way into this book—with clients' names changed of course.

As I shared my experiences—onstage, in seminars, and during keynotes—I started noticing something. Audiences were captivated. People wanted to know more. They were hungry for a deeper understanding of how their minds worked. And that's when it hit me... I had to write a book. Not just any book—a book that demystifies the unconscious mind and shows people how to take the driver's seat in their own lives.

That book is this book, **The Unconscious Authority**. And no, it's not just about hypnosis. It's about the incredible power of your mind, and how your present-day reactions, fears, habits, and decisions are often being driven by past-day experiences. Old programming you didn't ask for—and definitely didn't sign off on—is running the show. But the good news?

You can change the script.

Inside, you'll discover how your internal world—your thoughts, emotions, and beliefs—is not only separate from the chaos of the external world, but also way more influential than you think. You'll learn how to identify outdated programming, challenge it, and rewire your mental blueprint so you can finally stop living on autopilot and start living on purpose.

Oh, and given my comedy background, I'll make it all fun...

I hope you not only enjoy reading **The Unconscious Authority**, but that you actually use it. Put the principles into action. Start applying the tools. Test them out like a mad scientist in the lab of your own life. And when you see results (because you will), please send me a message. I want to hear your success stories—especially the weird ones. Those are my favorite!

Drop me an e-mail!

My Very Best To You,
Joe Hammer
Joe@UnconsciousAuthority.com

Finally, a Permanent Solution to Changing What is Invisibly Controlling You!

The Unconscious AUTHORITY

How to break through your mind's barriers, unleash your dormant wisdom and banish limitations in your life, relationships or career.

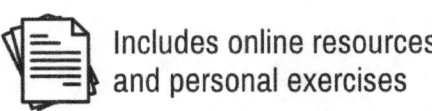

Includes online resources and personal exercises

Joe **Hammer**

A Note to the Reader

This book is about your mind. Not the part you use to remember where you left your keys (good luck with that), but the deeper part—the behind-the-scenes boss I like to call **The Unconscious Authority**. Think of it like your brain's stealthy middle manager... not flashy, not loud, but secretly running the show based on old programming from your past. And I do mean old—we're talking childhood wounds, awkward teenage moments, and that time your uncle told you money "doesn't grow on trees."

This inner boss has one job... *keep things familiar*. Even if "familiar" looks like self-sabotage, procrastination, dating emotionally unavailable people, or developing an allergic reaction to success. Yep, that's your Unconscious Authority, faithfully repeating what it learned way back when, whether or not it still makes sense.

This book dives into all of that. It explores why your mind is, well... fickle, moody and unpredictable. You'll find out why you sometimes do the exact opposite of what you actually want, why your belief system might be more like a "misbelief" system, and how all that internal wiring got installed in the first place—probably by someone who wasn't licensed.

I'll also be sharing some real-life stories from my hypnotherapy clients—everyday folks who decided they'd had enough of living with the same old problem. Some had been dealing with their issue for decades. Others showed up after one weird incident and said, "Nope. Not doing that again." The beauty is, once we got to the real root of the issue—not just putting a motivational Band-Aid on it—they saw powerful, fast, lasting change. No prescription meds. No years of lying on a couch talking about their dreams. Just deep mental work that actually stuck.

Here's the deal… we can't control the weather, the economy, or your neighbor's political opinions. But we can rewire the weird internal reactions that make us sabotage our goals, say the wrong thing at the worst time, or develop a sudden fear of success when opportunity knocks. (Yes, that's a thing.)

Ever reacted to something and immediately thought, "Why did I just do that?" Or found yourself stuck in yet another relationship that feels oddly familiar—but not in a good way? Or maybe you've got a habit that, no matter how many times you think you've cleaned it up, it keeps showing up in your life. That's not you being broken—it's just your Unconscious Authority running old software.

And don't worry, this book isn't just another "change your life with positive thinking" kind of book. If it were, you'd have already changed your life by now, right? It gets into the good stuff—like why change feels impossible even when you know exactly what you want. Why some self-help advice works for your friend but leaves you curled up in a blanket watching reruns of Charlie's Angels. Your Unconscious Authority has a say in all of that.

The Unconscious **Authority**

As a small business mentor, I've worked with a ton of brilliant entrepreneurs who couldn't figure out why they were stuck. They had the talent, the tools, and the vision—but zero traction. Once we cleared the old, crusty programming that was whispering things like "you're not good enough" or "this will never work," things moved. Fast. Suddenly, they were making bold moves, closing deals, and wondering why they ever doubted themselves in the first place.

Yes, we'll talk about hypnosis too—but not the movie kind where people get turned into assassins or cluck like chickens (unless you're into that). Hollywood has done a bang-up job of making hypnosis seem like spooky mind control. One classic film even blamed a hypnotist for orchestrating a murder—great for drama, terrible for public relations. Real hypnosis? Way more fascinating—and no one dies.

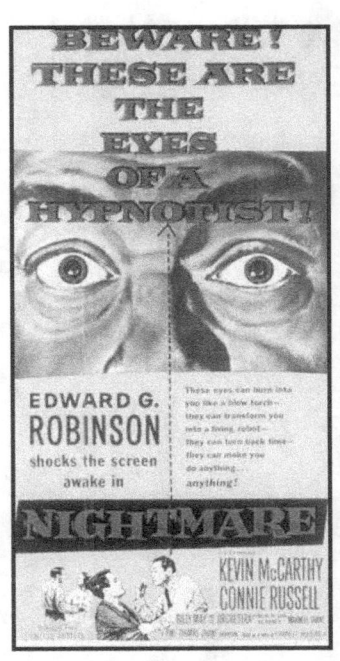

Hollywood's flamboyant, yet highly inaccurate depiction of hypnosis

At its core, this book is about you. It's about understanding the quiet force inside you that's been steering your ship (sometimes into rocky waters) and learning how to grab the wheel and say, "Thanks for your service, but I'll take it from here." It's about waking up from those unconscious "trances" you've been living in—patterns, habits, reactions—and choosing a better, more aligned way forward.

So buckle up. We're going to take a ride through the weird and wonderful terrain of your mind. There might be some bumps, some "aha!" moments, and a few mental gremlins to chase down—but I promise, you'll come out the other side with tools that work, stories that stick, and a stronger sense of who's really in charge up there.

Here's to upgrading your mental operating system and finally getting your Unconscious Authority to work for you instead of against you.

Introduction

Let's get one thing straight... this book isn't one of those fluffy self-help books that promises to change your life overnight if you just think positive, journal by candlelight, and visualize your way to a yacht.

Nope.

What you're about to learn actually works. And here's the beautiful part... it works without turning your life into a 24/7 boot camp of "inner work." Why? Because it's based on a scientific process. A process I've seen work with tons of clients—people just like you—who've kicked old behaviors to the curb without sweating through years of struggle.

Now, this isn't some new magical technique no one's ever heard of. In fact, you've already experienced this process in your life. You just didn't know what it was—or how to use it on purpose.

So, what's the big secret?

The **Unconscious Authority** (we'll just call it the "UA" from here on out, so my fingers don't get tired).

What Is the Unconscious Authority?

The UA is like that roommate who never talks, never cleans, and rearranges your entire life while you're asleep. It's the silent operator of your subconscious mind. It's been making decisions, forming habits, and guiding your behavior since... well, forever. And here's the fun part—it's doing all of this based on old beliefs, past experiences, and assumptions you probably don't even remember agreeing to.

It has:

- A voice (but you can't hear it),
- A plan (that you didn't approve),
- Immense power (with zero supervision),
- And absolutely no creativity.

It's like hiring a robot to manage your emotions, and then realizing it's been using a manual from 1987.

You are technically its boss. But it doesn't really listen to you. Not because it's rude—just because no one ever taught you how to give it proper instructions. And unless you do something about it, the UA will keep doing what it's always done, driving your life using yesterday's map and hoping it works out.

Now here's where it gets juicy.

The UA doesn't care if something is good or bad for you. It doesn't judge. It just executes. It's like electricity—it can power a cozy fireplace... or an electric chair. Totally depends on how it's being used. And most of us never read the user manual.

If you don't take the wheel, your UA will drive your life straight into patterns, habits, or relationships that feel weirdly famil-

The Unconscious **Authority**

iar—because, well, they are. It's repeating old scripts, most of which were written before you were old enough to spell "script."

Think of the UA like wind...

Imagine your life is a sailboat (stick with me here). The wind is your UA. It doesn't care where you're going. It doesn't care if you're headed for a beautiful tropical island or straight into a rock wall. It just blows.

If there's no one at the helm—or worse, someone who doesn't know how to steer—you're at the mercy of that wind. But give a skilled captain a map, a compass, and some solid sailing know-how, and now we've got progress. The wind hasn't changed—but how it's being used has.

That's what this book is all about.

We're going to hand you the map, teach you how to read the compass, and show you how to become the captain of your own mental ship. Because your UA isn't the enemy—it's just a powerful force waiting for direction.

If you don't learn to guide it, it'll keep taking you wherever it wants to go. But once you do learn how to work with it? You'll be amazed at how quickly your life starts shifting toward what you actually want.

So... ready to take the wheel?

Your State of Being ("Why Am I Like This?")

Let's be real—most people are walking around in a mild state of "what the hell is going on?" A quiet desperation, if you will. They're frustrated, anxious, and silently screaming into the void while smiling at the grocery store clerk. And let's not forget the mystery illnesses, the sleep problems, or that general feeling of "Is this all there is?"

Every single one of those experiences—good, bad, or "ugh"—can be traced back to actions that were quietly launched by your unconscious mind. Yep, that sneaky little puppeteer pulling the strings behind the curtain while you wonder why you just consumed an entire box of Oreos.

Meanwhile, the media is out here hypnotizing us 24/7, reminding us we're one wrinkle, one chin, or one hair out of place away from total social collapse. All while we're enjoying technology and luxuries that would've made our ancestors weep with joy.

A lot of the junk rattling around in your mind—those negative thought patterns, those unhelpful reactions, those why do I always do this? moments—were planted way back when you were a tiny, sponge-brained kid. You picked them up like mental hand-me-downs from parents, teachers, friends, and that one terrifying lady at the grocery store. Over time, those old experiences grew into full-blown beliefs and behaviors that now run on autopilot.

But let me be clear... those behaviors aren't you. They're not part of your personality. They're not your fate. They're mental

The Unconscious **Authority**

squatters—unwanted freeloaders who moved in rent-free, changed the locks, and are now bossing you around.

The good news? *You can evict them.*

All you need is the know-how to identify them, the desire to boot them out, and some better tenants to move in—like confidence, peace of mind, and maybe a little swagger.

Here's where people get tripped up... we've been taught to think emotions like happiness or fear are things that exist outside of us. That we have to chase them down or run away from them.

So we keep looking for the next thing that will "fix" us... a new job, a new partner, a new hairstyle, a 3-day juice cleanse (that most often ends in rage and a pizza). But the inner shift never really happens, because the problem isn't "out there." It's "in here"—in the programs that have been running the show since before we had a driver's license.

So why isn't all that external stuff fixing anything?

Because those pesky squatters are still in your head, throwing wild parties and putting cigarette burns in the carpet. Until we deal with them, nothing really changes. But you're in luck—this book is the eviction notice!

External Domain vs. Internal Dominion

"What's happening out there versus what's going on in here"

We're all living in two places at once—kind of like Airbnb-ing our brain.

Joe **Hammer**

First, there's the *External Domain*. That's the outside world... all the wild stuff happening to us. We're talking about traffic jams, surprise layoffs, your neighbor's yappy dog, your partner forgetting your birthday (again), or your favorite show getting cancelled right when it was getting good. It's a big ol' mess of circumstances, events, and drama—most of which we have zero control over. It just keeps coming whether you're ready or not.

Then there's the *Internal Dominion*. That's your inner world—the thoughts you think, the meaning you assign to stuff, and your reactions to all the madness swirling around in your External Domain. Unlike the chaos happening outside, this realm is 100% yours. You own it. You run the show. You're the mayor, the zoning commissioner, and the HOA president.

Your Unconscious Authority (UA)—that sneaky little mental gremlin we've been talking about—is the smooth-talking sales rep convincing you that your internal reactions are totally justified by whatever's happening externally. It's selling you on stress, fear, guilt, anger—basically a clearance rack of emotional clutter—and it's doing a great job because most of us are buying it without even realizing it.

Now, let's bring in a little science.

We all know the Law of Cause and Effect, right? For every action, there's an equal and opposite reaction. It's the backbone of quantum physics, the reason your coffee spills when you bump your elbow, and the explanation behind why toddlers lose it when you say "no" to their request for a Snickers bar.

The Unconscious **Authority**

This law applies to everything—from the tiniest cell in your body to the alignment of the planets. It's universal, constant, and not up for debate. Soooo...

Why on earth would we assume it doesn't apply to our thoughts? This is where we get into trouble...

We think the external world causes how we feel on the inside. Something happens out there, and boom—we're angry, anxious, or ready to scream into a throw pillow. We treat the External Domain like it has a remote control to our emotions. But in reality, it's our Internal Dominion—our interpretation, our thoughts, and our subconscious programming—that's flipping the emotional channels.

The bottom line is that external stuff is gonna happen. You can't stop it. But how you experience it? That's an inside job. And once you get wise to your UA and start calling the shots, everything changes!

The Creative Mind

Let's talk about that imaginative little rascal between your ears: your mind—aka your full-time, unpaid, overactive art director.

From the moment you popped into this world (and quite possibly before—depending on how far down the metaphysical rabbit hole you want to go), your mind has been painting vivid portraits of your life experiences. We're talking full-blown gallery exhibitions. Some are uplifting masterpieces that scream,

Joe **Hammer**

"You've got this!"... and others look like a toddler flung finger paint at a wall during a sugar crash. Welcome to the human condition.

The point is, your mind is always creating.

Always.

It doesn't take breaks. Even when you're "relaxing," it's back there humming like a Roomba vacuum in the dark, bumping into old memories and weird worries from 1986.

Despite all its chaos and drama, your mind is still plugged into something bigger, something wiser, something cosmic and cuddly (depending on how you like to reference the Universe, Source, God, Steve from accounting—no judgment here). This Higher Intelligence didn't show up just to mess with you. Its ultimate goal is...

Peace of Mind.

However, peace of mind doesn't just poof into existence like a magic trick. Nope. Change is a process. And that process looks a lot like digging a hole.

Let's break that down...

You think about the hole. You don't just randomly end up standing in one. You gotta want the hole. Really want it.

You decide on the specs. Where should this hole be? How wide? How deep? Is it a cozy firepit of transformation or a metaphorical escape tunnel from your current reality?

The Unconscious **Authority**

You grab a tool. A shovel, a spade, a backhoe... whatever. Point is, change needs tools.

You dig. One shovelful at a time. No shortcuts. No hiring a neighbor's friend who "used to be in construction." It's your hole. You dig it.

Now replace that "hole" with "your life" and "shovel" with "conscious awareness," and you'll start to see where we're going here.

You can't change what you don't acknowledge, and you can't direct what you haven't defined.

The Unconscious Authority, bless its stubborn little heart, is basically off doing its own thing with a bulldozer, rerouting your life toward outdated destinations. It's not malicious—it's just working off an old blueprint.

If you want to build something new, it's time to grab that shovel and update the blueprints. *The mind wants direction.* It's just been waiting for someone to come along and say, "Hey! Enough with the accidental life architecture—I'm taking over."

So, ready to roll up your sleeves and start digging?

Let's create a masterpiece!

The Master Recording Device (Your Brain on Autopilot)

Are you ready for a wild revelation? Here it is... your mind is the most advanced recording device ever invented. It's been record-

Joe Hammer

ing every single event, sensation, and emotional rollercoaster in your life since before you even knew what a juice box was.

And I mean *everything*.

That time you fell off your bike and cried in front of your crush? Logged.

When your teacher called you "average" in 4th grade? Logged.

Even that weird feeling you had walking into a room full of judgmental relatives—yep, also logged.

Further, your brain doesn't just record the facts, it also captures the "vibe" - the intensity of the moment. So, if you felt totally humiliated, your brain added a big fat emotional exclamation point to that memory.

And this around-the-clock, caffeinated record-keeper has no edit button.

None.

Not even a "delete" option or a "hey, maybe that wasn't so bad in hindsight" filter.

So a lot of those recordings are wildly dramatic. Some are even so intense they've been shoved into your brain's dusty subconscious because your conscious mind said, "Nope, don't want to deal with that mess."

But just because you don't remember them doesn't mean they're not still in there—lurking behind the scenes, whispering

The Unconscious **Authority**

outdated instructions to your Unconscious Authority like some rogue mission control crew.

And it's committed—working off childhood programming and carrying out missions you never approved, based on files that were written by people who may have been well-meaning but seriously under-qualified for brain software development.

"You're lazy."

"You're too sensitive."

"You're so special."

All of these totally unfiltered (and sometimes well-intentioned) labels were like little code snippets that your UA filed away for future use—without bothering to ask, "Hey, does this still apply when you're 35 and trying to start a business or have a healthy relationship?"

And yes, even the nice ones can mess with your wiring. Being told you're a "princess" or "gifted" sounds sweet, but it can come with invisible side effects like perfectionism, pressure to please, or the subconscious belief that the world owes you a tiara and a Disney soundtrack.

So what's the big takeaway?

Your outer world—the stress, the success, the love life, the job—is just a mirror of what's going on inside. And the UA? It's running the show on scripts written by toddlers and confused grown-ups.

But there is good news...

You're about to learn how to stop being the passenger in your own mind-movie and start directing your life story. Once you understand how this recording system works and how to send some of those bad tapes to the cutting room floor, you'll finally take charge of the rewriting process.

Grab some popcorn Grasshopper... It's time for a plot twist!

What Would You Like to Change in Your Life?

Let's be real—modern life feels like a game of emotional Jenga. We're juggling stress, tension, anxiety... and that one coworker who thinks forwarding chain emails is still a thing.

Most of that inner chaos isn't random. It's deeply rooted in old, emotional reactions to past experiences. Yep, it's our childhood programming showing up uninvited to the adult party again.

Your Unconscious Authority (UA) is like a helicopter parent that thinks it's doing you a favor—supervising every thought, guiding every move, and whispering, "Are you sure you're good enough to do that?" It's operating off outdated childhood software, and it's convinced it's "keeping you safe" by keeping you stuck.

Now, here's the good news... everything that has happened in your life had a purpose. I know, I know—cue the chorus of "everything happens for a reason" from well-meaning relatives and inspirational fridge magnets. But in this case, they're actually right. All the ups, the downs, the awkward breakups, the

The Unconscious **Authority**

failed attempts, the health scares—they've handed you the exact toolkit you need to grow. The Universe, clever as ever, knows what it's doing—even when it feels like you've been handed a pop quiz on a subject you never studied.

So here you are. You want to make some changes. Real ones. Lasting ones. The kind that stick around longer than your New Year's gym membership. I don't need to know what they are (though I'd love to hear them if you're sharing). Whether it's finally having that difficult conversation, ditching a limiting belief, improving your finances, getting over the fear of speaking in public, or forgiving someone who did you dirty—your change is valid.

Let's talk forgiveness for a second. It's one of those things that sounds super spiritual and mature, but deep down you might still want to throw a shoe at the person who wronged you.

Forgiveness is one of the most misunderstood yet powerful tools available to those seeking freedom from emotional pain, resentment, and regret. Contrary to popular belief, forgiveness is not about excusing bad behavior, condoning harm, or forgetting what happened. It's not a sign of weakness, and it certainly doesn't mean you have to reconcile with someone who hurt you. Forgiveness is about one thing, *your peace*. It's a personal decision to release the emotional grip that past pain holds over your present life.

When we hold on to anger or resentment, we don't trap the person who hurt us—we trap ourselves. The emotional charge from old wounds festers in the subconscious, influencing how we view others, how we react to stress, and even how we view ourselves. This often manifests in recurring life patterns: failed relationships, chronic anxiety, low self-worth, or an inability to trust. Until the emotional root is uncovered and released, these patterns continue to loop. Forgiveness is a key that unlocks that loop.

In hypnotherapy, forgiveness work can be especially powerful. Because hypnosis allows access to our Unconscious Authority, we can go directly to the source of unresolved pain. Under guided trance, you can revisit past events in a safe, non-retraumatizing way, often viewing them from a more compassionate and empowered perspective. From there, forgiveness is not a forced intellectual exercise; it becomes a natural emotional release.

Sometimes the person needing forgiveness isn't someone else—it's ourselves. Self-forgiveness is a crucial yet often overlooked aspect of healing. Whether it's guilt over past mistakes, shame from perceived failures, or a general sense of unworthiness, self-directed anger can be just as toxic as resentment toward others. In hypnosis, you can gently confront these inner judgments and rewrite the story you've been telling yourself, often emerging with greater compassion and self-acceptance.

It's also important to recognize that forgiveness doesn't always happen all at once. It's a process, and in many cases, a layered one. You might forgive intellectually, then emotionally, and finally, behaviorally—meaning you no longer react from the wound. Hypnotherapy allows this process to unfold organically, without forcing or rushing it. The subconscious works on its own timeline, and hypnosis honors that rhythm.

Forgiveness, at its core, is a decision to stop giving the past permission to shape the present. And that decision opens up space for new beliefs, healthier relationships, and a more authentic version of self. Without forgiveness, personal growth is often superficial or incomplete—because we're still dragging around the emotional residue of old wounds. When that baggage is released, the transformation is not just mental or emotional—it's felt in the body, spirit, and even behavior.

Once forgiveness has been integrated in a hypnosis session, clients often describe a sense of lightness, clarity, and peace. They don't just think differently—they feel different. That shift is what makes forgiveness so central to deep inner work. It's not just a spiritual or moral principle—it's a practical, therapeutic necessity for anyone serious about true personal change.

In the end, forgiveness is freedom. Not for the one who wronged you—but for you. It's not a favor to them. It's a gift to yourself. And in the hands of a skilled hypnotherapist, it becomes one of the most transformative tools for releasing the past and reclaiming your life. Now, you've probably tried a few things already:

Motivational seminars? Check.

Self-help books with overly enthusiastic authors? Check.

Walked barefoot across hot coals? Double check.

And still... the change you crave keeps dodging your efforts.

But fear not—this book's approach is different. You're not about to get a to-do list full of exhausting mental pushups. Instead, you're going to learn a kind of mental technology that doesn't require massive effort or chanting under a full moon (unless that's your thing). Once you understand how your UA has been running the show, you'll be able to gently (and effectively) take the wheel.

So, are you ready to make that change feel less like a grind and more like a shift? Fantastic. Let's roll!

Ink It (Seriously, Grab a Pen...)

Alright, let's kick things off with the single most powerful (yet strangely underrated) move you can make... writing down what you want to change. That's right—put pen to paper.

There's something magical—like wizard-level magical—about writing down your goals, dreams, or that nagging habit you want to show the exit door. When you take your thoughts and make them tangible by putting them into words, you're already halfway to turning them into reality.

So... what exactly would you like to change in your life?

Be specific. Be bold. Be honest. Write it down. This isn't a throwaway journaling exercise. You'll be coming back to this list later. It's your personal treasure map!

The Unconscious **Authority**

Please return your seatback to its upright position and secure your tray table. This personal growth journey is taking off, and there may be a few bumps as we fly through old patterns and limiting beliefs. But don't worry—we'll serve snacks.

The Unconscious Authority— your brain's uninvited micromanager—has been whispering nonsense for years... stuff like "you're not enough" or "change is hard" or "maybe just one more cookie before we get serious." Those thoughts? Not helpful. Not true. And not welcome anymore.

What you're about to discover is how that inner voice—your UA—has been making some pretty questionable calls without your permission. It means well, but let's be honest, its track record is a little spotty.

You'll start to see how people from your past—your parents, teachers, that one friend who said you "talk too much"—all left behind a little mind debris. It's like emotional glitter: hard to see, even harder to clean up, and somehow still clinging to everything years later. And while you may have consciously forgotten a lot of those early experiences, your UA has not. Oh no. It's been keeping notes. And it's been using those notes to shape how you see the world, how you behave, and even how you react when someone leaves you on "read."

You're also going to realize how your UA has quietly been working overtime to keep things safe and predictable in your life—even if "safe and predictable" looks a lot like "stuck and frustrated." It wants you to stay in your comfort zone.

We'll also pull back the curtain on how your perceptions, beliefs, and assumptions have been crafting your reality. Everything you experience is filtered through what you believe to be true... even when what you believe is absolute nonsense.

I'll walk you through the three big players in your mind—your conscious mind, your subconscious mind, and of course, our troublemaker-in-chief, the UA. You'll finally get why they sometimes feel like they're all in a group chat without you. And once you understand how they operate? *Game Changer*.

Oh, and then there's the good stuff... the 7 Mind Maxims. These are the unbreakable, always-in-play laws that govern how your mind works. Don't worry, they're not as boring as they sound. Think of them as cheat codes for being human.

You'll also meet a few of my real-life clients—people who were struggling with everything from fear to bad habits to toxic relationships—until they learned how to lovingly evict their UA from the driver's seat. The stories are inspiring, relatable, and most importantly, real. No staged testimonials or dramatic infomercials here.

Finally, you'll learn how to rewrite your UA's faulty programming. You'll discover a process that lets you strip out the emotional static, unplug from the old crap, and start giving your mind some upgraded instructions. You'll stop reacting on autopilot and start creating a life that actually feels like yours.

So whether you're looking to heal a relationship, drop a habit, make more money, level up your career, or finally stop sweating

The Unconscious **Authority**

through your shirt during public speaking—you're only about 30 days away from a life that makes sense and feels good.

Let me say this with love... *don't be a wimp.*

Seriously. This stuff works. I tell my clients to approach this process like they're planning the vacation of a lifetime. You know that energy you get before a trip.

The UA couldn't care less how that stuff affects your life today. It has zero interest in whether you're happy, fulfilled, or stress-free. Its job is just to keep delivering the same familiar junk because familiar = safe in its opinion.

However, you're about to learn how to cancel that subscription.

You'll discover how to break up with those outdated emotional patterns, release the tension that's been tagging along with your old experiences, and finally stop reacting like your buttons are being mashed by an sugar-high induced 2 year old. Once you're freed from that mess, you'll respond to life from a whole new place—one that's aligned with who you actually want to be.

Now, let's talk commitment.

Any real change in life requires one very important thing: *commitment*. The kind where you actually do the work, not just think about it while watching inspirational TED Talks with a bowl of Ben & Jerry's.

So I have to ask... are you in?

Joe **Hammer**

My Desired Life Changes

The Unconscious **Authority**

Are you really, truly ready to stop circling the same emotional cul-de-sac and finally drive toward the life you want?

Yes? Good!

So this is your line in the sand. No more waiting, no more blaming, no more someday-maybe-later. It's time to stop hoping and start knowing. And the truth is, you already have everything you need inside you to shift your life in the direction you actually want to go.

You've got a built-in mechanism—like spiritual GPS meets emotional Swiss Army knife—that's been patiently waiting for you to learn how to use it.

This book? It's the instruction manual.

Now ink it. Your future self is already high-fiving you.

 This symbol indicates a written assignment you must do before proceeding.

 This symbol indicates a downloadable file to assist you in the exercise.

Download exercise forms here:
at www.UnconsciousAuthority.com/forms

… Joe **Hammer**

What You'll Learn

Alright, let's get something straight right off the bat—you don't need a psychology degree or a meditation retreat in the Himalayas to make powerful changes in your life. What you do need is a working understanding of your Unconscious Authority. It's that part of your mind that's been steering the ship behind the scenes.

And just like a boat captain doesn't need to know everything about meteorology to sail—he just needs to know how to work the wind—you don't need to become a mind expert to change the trajectory of your life. You just need to learn how to work with your wind (the UA), rather than constantly getting knocked overboard by it.

What you're about to discover is how that inner voice has been making some pretty questionable calls without your permission. It means well, but let's be honest, its track record is a little rocky.

You'll start to see how people from your past—your parents, teachers, that one friend who said you "talk too much"—all left behind a little mind debris. It's like emotional glitter… hard to see, even harder to clean up, and somehow still clinging to everything years later. And while you may have consciously forgotten a lot of those early experiences, your UA has not. It's been keeping notes. And it's been using those notes to shape how you see the world, how you behave, and even how you react.

The Unconscious **Authority**

You're also going to realize how your UA has quietly been working overtime to keep things safe and predictable in your life—even if "safe and predictable" looks a lot like "stuck and frustrated." *It wants you to stay in your comfort zone.*

We'll also pull back the curtain on how your perceptions, beliefs, and assumptions have been crafting your reality. Everything you experience is filtered through what you believe to be true... even when what you "believe" is absolute nonsense.

I'll walk you through the three big players in your mind—your conscious mind, your subconscious mind, and of course, our troublemaker-in-chief, the UA. You'll finally get why they sometimes feel like they're all in a group chat without you. And you'll understand how they operate.

Oh, and then there's the 7 Mind Maxims. These are the unbreakable, always-in-play laws that govern how your mind works. Don't worry, they're not as boring as they sound. Think of them as cheat codes for being human.

You'll also meet a few of my real-life clients—people who were struggling with everything from fear to bad habits to toxic rela-

---

WARNING:
By ignoring, dismissing, or skimming the exercises and content of this book without fully engaging as recommended, you surrender control to the unconscious forces driving your life's "status quo." Don't let that happen—seize this opportunity to break free and shape your future with intention!

tionships—until they learned how to lovingly evict their UA from the driver's seat. The stories are inspiring, relatable, and most importantly, real. No staged testimonials or dramatic infomercials here.

Finally, you'll learn how to rewrite your UA's faulty programming. You'll discover a process that lets you strip out the emotional static, unplug from the old crap, and start giving your mind some upgraded instructions. You'll stop reacting on autopilot and start creating a life that actually feels like yours.

So whether you're looking to heal a relationship, drop a habit, make more money, level up your career, or finally stop sweating during public speaking—you're only 30 days away from a life that makes sense and feels good.

Let me say this with love... *don't be a wimp.*

Seriously. This stuff works. I tell my clients to approach this process like they're planning the vacation of a lifetime. You know that energy you get before a trip—the excitement, the clarity, the sense of "let's make this amazing"? Channel that right here. You've got this.

And I got your back...

Okay Little Buddy, It's Time to Get to Work

Before you start high-fiving your future self, let's get real about what lasting change actually takes. It's more than a vision board and affirmations on your bathroom mirror.

The Unconscious **Authority**

To make lasting changes in your life, you have to do three things:

- Understand how and why you got where you are (stop blaming your ex, your boss, or Mercury in retrograde).
- Learn how to get out of that space and move forward
- Actually begin the practice of steering yourself where you want to go.

Now, let's talk about two very important characters who'll be joining us on this ride... the subconscious mind and your shady but predictable roommate, the Unconscious Authority (UA).

Think of your subconscious mind as a giant storage closet. It's crammed full of all your past thoughts, beliefs, emotions, and weird childhood memories you thought were long gone. You know, the emotional equivalent of that ugly sweater from 7th grade you've been subconsciously wearing ever since.

The UA is your personal warehouse manager. It doesn't ask questions. It doesn't judge. It doesn't even clock out for lunch. It just pulls from the subconscious storage closet and starts handing stuff to you on autopilot. Over and over. Forever. Until you tell it to knock it off.

And the UA couldn't care less how that stuff affects your life today. It has zero interest in whether you're happy, fulfilled, or stress-free. Its job is just to keep delivering the same familiar junk because, in its opinion, "familiar equals safe."

But the good news is that you're about to learn how to cancel that subscription.

Joe **Hammer**

You'll discover how to break up with those outdated emotional patterns, release the tension that's been tagging along with your old experiences, and finally stop over-reacting. Once you're freed from that mess, you'll respond to life from a whole new place—one that's aligned with who you actually want to be.

Now, let's talk commitment.

Any real change in life requires one very important thing: *commitment*. The kind where you actually do the work, not just think about it while watching inspirational TED Talks with a bowl of Ben & Jerry's.

So I have to ask... are you in?

Are you really, truly ready to stop circling the same emotional cul-de-sac and finally drive toward the life you want?

Yes?

Good! Now COMMIT!

Commitment is what transforms a promise into a reality...
Commitment is the stuff character is made of; the power to change the
face of things. It is the daily triumph of integrity over skepticism.
Abraham Lincoln

Commitment Proclamation

Yes, Joe, I am totally committed to making the powerful changes I truly desire in my life. (And I solemnly swear not to ghost myself halfway through this book.)

X_____

[Your Signature Here]

Signed this ____ day of _____, 20____

JOE'S NOTE ON: VALIDATION

The ego doesn't care if it's a terrible idea, it just wants applause for having one

The ego has a relentless hunger for validation, regardless of the quality of the idea or decision it's attached to. It's a frustrating aspect of human behavior. The ego isn't interested in logic, or outcomes, it just wants to be seen, heard, and celebrated. Once it latches onto a concept - no matter how poorly thought out - it will go to great lengths to protect it, defend it, and parade it around. It's a disaster in disguise, and it's always noticed by most everyone else.

In relationships, this kind of ego-driven thinking can be especially destructive. It's someone who insists on being "right" even when it costs them the connection with their partner. They might double down on a bad opinion, a petty argument, or an emotional outburst just to avoid feeling wrong. Instead of focusing on a resolution or compromise, the ego uses the situation to feed its personal narrative of superiority or victimhood. The result is most always unnecessary conflict, emotional distance, and missed opportunities for true connections… many times, resulting in avoidance.

In business, ego validation can lead one to flawed strategies, ignore critical feedback, or shut down innovative ideas that didn't originate from them. It's the classic "my way or the highway" mindset, where a team's success is thwarted by one person's need to be the "smartest" or "right."

CHAPTER ONE
The Formation of Our Reality

Illusions, Perceptions, and Beliefs—Oh My!

Before we dive headfirst into the fascinating tech (and the occasional weird quirks) of the human mind, we need to talk about the trio that's been secretly shaping your reality this whole time... *illusions, perceptions,* and *beliefs*. Think of them as the behind-the-scenes production team of your mental Broadway show.

Illusions

Picture this... You're sitting in a well-lit theater, popcorn and soda in hand. Out steps a magician—the kind who oozes confidence. There's nothing on stage but a skinny black table. Suddenly, his glamorous assistant struts out.

With a dramatic wave of his hand, she closes her eyes and lies down. Another wave and—boom!—she's levitating. Just floating there. Defying gravity.

Then he grabs a steel hoop and passes it around her body, proving this glorious feat is legit. And you, sitting there with your jaw in your lap, cannot for the life of you figure out how the heck this is happening.

Joe **Hammer**

That, my friend, is an illusion—something that seems impossible, but is really just physics and some very sneaky stage engineering.

You're living your life with the exact same kind of illusions. But instead of prestidigitation, it's your thoughts doing the magic show.

See, your thoughts can play tricks on you too—except in this case, you are the magician, and the assistant, and the audience. You're not seeing yourself as the infinite being you truly are. Nope. You're seeing the version of you that's been conditioned, edited, Photoshopped, and stuffed into a neat little mental box marked, "This Is Just Who I Am."

That version is a trick. A very convincing one, but a trick nonetheless.

Like the magician's levitation act, your sense of self is often just the result of some clever behind-the-scenes wiring—beliefs you inherited, perceptions you were fed, and illusions you bought into before you even knew how to spell "self-awareness."

The good news? You don't need to become a master illusionist to reveal what's real. You just need to understand how the trick works... and maybe be willing to walk backstage once in a while.

What you think you see in the mirror is not all you are. Not even close. You are so much more—and you don't need a magician's top hat and cape to prove it.

The Unconscious **Authority**

Reality is merely an illusion, albeit a very persistent one.
Albert Einstein

Perceptions: The Funhouse Mirrors of the Mind

Perception is that sneaky little brain app that takes reality, runs it through our personal filters, and spits out whatever the heck it wants. It's like your mind's own iPhone filter—only instead of dog ears or soft lighting, it's got childhood experiences and emotional baggage.

Perception is how we translate the world through our own internal lens. Some of those lenses are clean and rosy, others are foggy and cracked. The point is, we all see the world a little differently, and that's not a flaw—it's just how our brain works.

Ever tell someone something exciting, only to have them look at you like you just announced you were packing up your stuff and joining a circus?

You say, "I just got a new job! I'm so pumped!"

And they comae back at you with, "Hmm, well, hope your new boss isn't a micromanager. And watch out for office politics."

Thanks, Karen. Super helpful.

Or maybe you shared a messy moment with a friend, like, "I locked my keys in the car, it started raining, and then I dropped my phone in a puddle." And they say, "Yeah, but at least you're safe, and maybe this was the Universe slowing you down."

One of you is seeing storm clouds, the other is spotting rainbows. Neither of you is necessarily right or wrong—you're just looking through different windows.

Kinda like that classic Peanuts moment...

Lucy's staring out the window and says, "What a beautiful day, Charlie Brown! The sky is blue, the grass is green, the birds are singing—life is good!"

And Charlie Brown responds with, "I see spots on the glass."

Boom. That's perception in a nutshell.

Charlie's not wrong. Lucy's not wrong. They're just rocking their own inner weather forecasts. And you? You've got yours too.

Your perception becomes your reality. Not *the* reality—*your* reality. And the sooner we understand that, the sooner we can start scrubbing those mental windows and changing the view.

Because let's be real... no one wants to go through life only seeing smudges on the glass, right?

Beliefs – The Invisible Puppet-Masters

Alright, now that we've ruffled the curtains on illusions and perceptions, let's step into the backstage VIP lounge of your mind—*beliefs*. These bad boys are the real power players. They're like the directors of a play you didn't even know you auditioned for, quietly shouting stage directions into your mental

The Unconscious **Authority**

earpiece: "You're not good enough!" ... "Act awkward at the party!" ... "Just eat the donut, Susan, life is meaningless!"

Beliefs are often planted early on, like weird little seeds tossed in your mental garden by parents, teachers, culture, or that one time your cousin told you you'd never make it as a dancer. (and now look at you... you're not a dancer).

Beliefs don't need to be true to be powerful. They just need you to believe in them.

Take, for instance, that timeless crowd favorite: "When I win the lottery..."

Ah yes, the ol' fantasy-fueled Band-Aid. You've probably heard it (or said it), followed by something like:

"...I'll travel the world."

"...I'll finally be happy."

Whatever the dream, it rests on a massive IF—and when that magical lotto moment doesn't arrive (statistically, it won't), people sink back into their "see-I-knew-it" slump. Their inner narrator says, "Nice try, pal. Back to the grind. And don't forget to feel disappointed, again."

Belief, my friend, is a double-edged sword. When misused, it cuts you off from progress and reinforces failure.

There was a study comparing the life outcomes of college grads versus high school grads, and the college kids absolutely crushed it. But it wasn't because they remembered their Business Economics 101 notes. It was because they believed they were valuable, destined for success, and worthy of more. Their degrees were less "knowledge bombs" and more like golden tickets of self-importance. Confidence, not content, changed their lives.

Now, buckle up for a strange and dark example of belief power...

A European prison inmate, sentenced to death, agreed to participate in a scientific study. He was told he'd be slowly bled out as a method of execution. The setup? A small, harmless cut... some flowing water next to his arm... and a carefully rigged "drip, drip, drip" into a bucket that he thought was his lifeblood leaking away.

He couldn't see it—but he could hear it, feel it, and most of all... believe it.

Doctors whispered things like, "He's losing a lot of blood..." and "His pulse is fading..."

And guess what? The guy actually died. Not because he lost blood—but because he believed he was dying.

Belief is powerful, whether it's lifting you up or holding you back.

And yes—belief works the other way, too.

Ever know someone who just seems magically lucky? Like they sneeze and end up with a promotion or "accidentally" find a $100 bill in their coat pocket?

You start wondering, "Do they have some secret code to life I missed while I was binge-watching bad reality TV?"

Well, the truth is—they *believe* they're lucky. And that belief changes their actions, their confidence, their energy... even how others respond to them.

They walk into the room like good things are supposed to happen. And sometimes? The Universe shrugs and says, "Sure, why not."

I remember being a kid and watching my mom stroll over to a patch of clovers. Without breaking a sweat—she'd pluck a four-leaf clover like it was just sitting there waving at her. No fuss. No muss. Meanwhile, I'd be ten feet away, hunched over like a lawn detective, combing through clovers for what felt like a week. Nothing. Zilch. Just a sore neck and a growing suspicion that four-leaf clovers were a government hoax, or only visible to single mothers.

Whether it's making you shrink or shine, belief is always working. The question is—are you letting it work for you, or against you?

Stay tuned. We're just getting warmed up.

Luck? Who Says?

Let's have a quick chat about this so-called "luck." Who decided a four-leaf clover was lucky? Why is breaking a mirror supposed to curse you with seven years of bad luck? And why is a rabbit's foot lucky? I mean... it clearly wasn't for the rabbit.

These "lucky" or "unlucky" objects have no magical power on their own. None. Zilch. The only magic they have is the magic

Joe Hammer

we assign to them in our minds. It's all about belief. If you think breaking a mirror will bring bad luck, your Unconscious Authority will grab that idea and run with it like it just got drafted to the NFL.

I remember going to bingo with my mom as a kid. Now, Mom was not just a player—she was a bingo gladiator. While most people used bingo chips, she brought a tin of pennies to the table. And in that tin with the pennies was her prized possession... a tiny, one-inch naked plastic baby doll. This little thing had one job—be her good luck charm.

Whenever she needed a number to win, her friends would yell, "Put your baby on it, Josie!" And she did. Every time. And she won a lot. Was it the power of the plastic baby? I doubt it. I think the Universe just had a soft spot for a single mom doing her best to provide for her kids. Her desire was aligned with need, not greed. That's a recipe the Universe seems to love.

Now, if you've been to one of my Mind Extension workshops, you know I do something a little unconventional when you complete the workshop... you walk under a ladder to get your certificate. Why? Because we like to break mental patterns. People hesitate... some even tiptoe like they're entering a haunted house... but guess what? Nobody exploded. No bad luck followed. We're still here, thriving.

The bottom line is that there's no such thing as luck. There is, however, a very real, very loving Universe just waiting to hand

The Unconscious **Authority**

you the goods—if your mind is in alignment. Even when the "gifts" look like dumpster fires, they usually carry the lesson we needed most.

And please, don't try to micromanage the Universe. It doesn't take orders. Your job is to get clear on what you want, align your energy and thoughts with that desire, and then trust your UA to handle the logistics. It will and it always does.

There's an old Latin proverb that says, "Believe you have it, and you have it." And it's true. Have you ever met a salesperson who's got zero client appointments but somehow manages to "squeeze you in" next Tuesday at 3:15? That's belief in action. That's someone living in the "as if" moment.

Your UA loves "as if" scenarios. During my stage hypnosis shows, I tell participants to act "as if" they're flirting with Leonardo DiCaprio or sobbing uncontrollably at the sight of Taylor Swift. And they do it. Like Oscar-worthy performances. Why? Because belief—even pretend belief—sends a strong signal to the subconscious mind. And that signal creates results.

Take a moment to look around. The chair you're sitting on? Someone believed it could exist. The phone you're texting on? Same deal. These are real-world manifestations of someone's thought plus belief combo.

Beliefs are powerful little critters. They're like invisible architects building the framework of your life. But they can be sneaky too—because many of them were installed in your brain without your consent. Some noble, some not-so-much.

Joe **Hammer**

Beliefs are stubborn. They hide behind habits, protected by your subconscious like a guard dog with a fresh bone. They feel right, even when they're dead wrong.

For example, I once ran into an old acquaintance at a store. She told me I hadn't changed in 15 years and asked me what my "secret" was for staying fit and relaxed. I started talking about meditation, clean eating, hot yoga... and mid-sentence she cut me off with, "Oh, forget it, I can't do any of that." And she's right.

The world we see that seems so insane is the result of a belief system that is not working. To perceive the world differently, we must be willing to change our belief system, let the past slip away, expand our sense of now, and dissolve the fear in our minds.
William James
American philosopher, psychologist

Not because she can't, but because her beliefs say she can't. Her UA is working overtime to reinforce that script.

Your beliefs don't just reflect your reality, *they create it*. And they didn't come from nowhere. They came from past experiences, culture, family, and sometimes that third-grader who told you your head was shaped like a cantaloupe.

Take food, for example. Imagine you're invited to dinner in South Korea. The main course is... dog. You hesitate. "Where I'm from, we don't eat dogs," you say.

But your host replies, "Oh, these aren't pets—these are food dogs." [1]

The Unconscious **Authority**

Now flip the scene... you serve a beautiful filet mignon to your Hindu friend visiting from India. They refuse to eat it because, to them, cows are sacred. [2]

Who's right? Neither. It's not about "right" or "wrong"—it's about *beliefs*.

Even a kid's hatred of broccoli usually isn't about broccoli—it's because Dad once said, "Ugh, that stuff's gross," and the UA took notes.

Our thoughts, attitudes and beliefs we hold today are quietly and forcefully shaping our tomorrow.
Joe Hammer

Our lives are full of these sneaky, limiting beliefs:

"I can't write."

"I'm not talented."

"I'll always be overweight."

"I'm not smart enough."

"I'm afraid of flying."

---

[1] Although outlawed in the '80s, there has been virtually no regulation of the technically illegal dog meat industry in Korea, and the government turns a blind eye. This has led to allegations of horrible conditions at dog farms and slaughterhouses.

[2] The Hindu faith believes the cow is a symbol of the earth, the nourisher; the ever-giving undemanding provider. It represents life and the sustenance of life. They say, "The cow is so generous, taking nothing but water, grass, and grain, it gives and gives of it milk as does the liberated soul give of its spiritual knowledge."

Joe **Hammer**

All of these came from somewhere. And in many cases, from people who loved us—they just passed along their own fears and limitations.

Now, let's flip the script.

You, my friend, are about to rewrite the code. These beliefs came from historical programming; in many cases from those we love and actually meant the very best for us.

My Bread Crust Story

Let's talk about bread crust. I don't like it. Never have. I know—scandalous.

When I'm at a nice restaurant, and they bring out that warm, fresh bread, I go straight for the soft, fluffy center like a carb-seeking missile. The crust? Left behind like the outer layer of a rejected croissant. Weird, right? Because technically, it's all the same bread. Same ingredients, same oven, same overall vibe. So why the crust discrimination?

Well, the mystery of my crust-aversion was solved in one of the most unexpected places.. a regressive hypnosis session. Yep, during my hypnotherapy training, my lunch buddy noticed my odd anti-crust behavior and offered to take my subconscious mind on a little field trip. Destination? The first moment of crust-related trauma.

Pow! I was five years old, sitting at the kitchen table, sunburned from playing outside, chowing down on a sandwich that I had artistically eaten by leaving only the crust behind.

The Unconscious **Authority**

Enter Mom, cheerfully saying, "Joey, eat your crust, it'll make your hair curly!"

Seems innocent enough, right? Just a classic parental fib, like "if you swallow gum, it'll stay in your stomach for seven years," or "Santa's watching." But my UA was not having it. Nope. The second she said "curly hair," my brain's hard drive spun back to a classmate named Zach.

Now, Zach had curls. A lot of them. He also had a less than desirable scent. He came from a rough background, and personal grooming clearly wasn't high on the family's to-do list. His hair was a tangled and matted. And in that moment, five-year-old me connected the dots...

Crust = Curly Hair = I become Zach = No thanks.

My UA immediately installed a mental firewall: "No crust, ever." And just like that, my life as a crust-refuser was born.

Does bread crust actually make your hair curly? No. Do I know that now? Of course. Did my mom mean well? Absolutely. But that innocent comment got hijacked by the UA and rerouted into the "Danger! Unwanted Outcome" folder.

You see, it doesn't matter if something is logical or scientifically accurate. If your subconscious believes it, it's as good as gospel. And it doesn't stop at bread crust.

Let's go back to that "dog for dinner" scenario. If your stomach flipped a little at the thought, that's not your taste buds talking—it's your beliefs. You were programmed to see dogs as companions, not cuisine. Meanwhile, you're probably totally fine with eating a cow. Unless, of course, you're a fellow vegetarian, in which case—high five, kale buddy!

These conflicting beliefs don't exist because we made rational choices after thorough contemplation. No. They were handed to us. Like hand-me-down pants, but for the brain.

In his book *Animal Liberation,* philosopher Peter Singer calls this phenomenon *speciesism* (There's also a thought-provoking documentary by Mark Devries by the same name, if you're into deep dives about the ethics of food. And guilt. Lots of guilt.)

Back to beliefs... The hamburger didn't come into your life because you made a philosophical decision about food. It was put in front of you, someone said, "Eat it," and you did. Then your brain filed it under "Delicious and Totally Normal," and that was that. Belief installed.

Your beliefs are your reality.

Not your facts. Not your logic. Your beliefs. If your UA believes the crust turns you into Zach, guess what? You're tossing crusts until your dying day.

What's really standing in the way of the changes you say you want? I'm talking about those dreams, goals, and fresh new habits that look amazing in your head but somehow keep ghosting you in real life. It's easy to blame timing, the economy, or your co-worker sleeping with the boss, but let's zoom in a little closer. There's usually something sneakier at play—like a belief or a subconscious script that's been running the show behind your back.

The Unconscious **Authority**

Your current reality? It's not random. It's built on layers of historic programming—some of it loving, some of it laughably outdated, and some of it completely sabotaging your progress.

We all carry with us a mental blueprint or picture of ourselves. It has been built up from our own beliefs about ourselves. But most of these beliefs about ourselves have unconsciously been formed from our past experience, our successes and failures, our humiliations, our triumphs, and the way other people have related to us, especially in early childhood. From all these we mentally construct a "self" (or a picture of a self). Once an idea or a belief about ourselves goes into this picture it becomes "true" as far as we personally are concerned. We do not question its validity, but proceed to act upon it just as if it were true.
Maxwell Maltz, Author

So here's the mission... look at your life as it is today, especially in the areas where you feel stuck or frustrated. Think about the things you want to change. What old programming could be keeping you from moving forward? You might not have an answer right away—and that's totally fine. This isn't a pop quiz. Just sit with the questions. Let stuff float to the surface. Don't dismiss the odd or insignificant memories. Sometimes the seemingly random things are the ones holding the biggest emotional charge.

Take notes. Reflect. Sleep on it. Give your subconscious a chance to speak up.

Now, in the next section of the book, there's a set of questions waiting for you—your first real deep dive. This isn't busywork, it's groundwork. These questions are part of your personal excavation process, and they're key to building what I call your *Subconscious Motivation Worksheets* later on.

This is the stuff that will help you start identifying the illusions, perceptions, and beliefs that have been setting your internal GPS—often in the exact opposite direction of where you want to go.

Illusions

Think of illusions as those things you tell yourself are flat-out impossible—even though, deep down, a little part of you knows they're totally doable. You might have convinced yourself that a certain goal is way out of reach, but if we dig a little, you'll probably find the only thing stopping you is an outdated belief planted there by someone else, somewhere back in the day.

Perceptions

Then there are perceptions—the things that seem hard, but aren't really impossible. Like public speaking. Or going to the gym without having a full-blown panic attack. These are the things that feel like a grind but could be conquered with a mindset shift and maybe a decent playlist.

Beliefs

And then there are your beliefs. The real drivers. These are the deeply rooted thoughts that formed when you were just a little

The Unconscious **Authority**

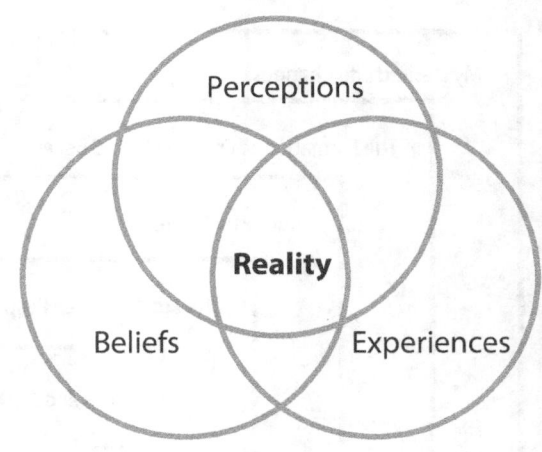

sponge of a human, soaking up the opinions of your parents, teachers, friends, and probably a few cartoon characters. Most of your beliefs were passed on without your permission, and now they're running the background software of your adult life. Some are helpful. Others... not so much.

For example, you may consciously want to lose weight, start a new business, or fall in love again. But if your belief system is quietly humming a tune like "I'm not good enough" or "Nothing ever works out for me," guess what? You'll keep replaying that reality.

So yes, in this part of the book I'm asking you to do a little inner digging. Not the sexiest thing in the world, I know. But it's absolutely essential if you want to stop being held hostage by outdated mental files and start living a life that actually aligns with what you want.

Grab a pen. Open the forms. Sit with yourself.

Write down whatever pops up. And remember—there's no such thing as a wrong answer. Only real ones.

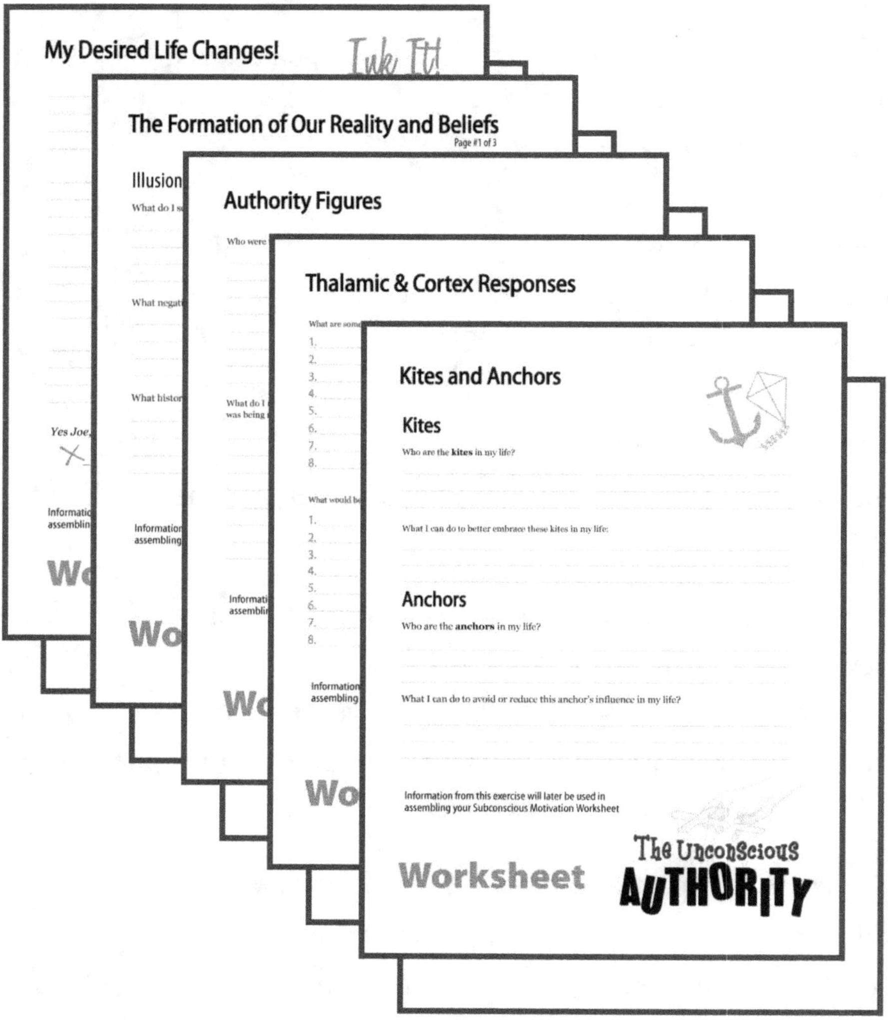

Joe **Hammer**

Subconscious Motivation Worksheets

Download the forms now at:
www.UnconsciousAuthority.com/forms

The Formation of Our Reality and Beliefs

Illusions

What do I see as impossible, even though at a deeper level I know it to be real and achievable?

What negative thoughts do I hold about this illusion?

What historic programming from others do I hold about it?

Perceptions

What do I perceive as difficult, yet at a deeper level know it is achievable?

What negative thoughts do I hold about these perceptions?

What historic programming from others do I hold about it?

Beliefs

What is the history of my beliefs as they relate to the change I desire?

What negative thoughts do I hold about these beliefs?

What historic programming from others do I hold about them?

Form: *The Formation of Our Reality and Beliefs*
Download this exercise form at www.UnconsciousAuthority.com/forms

JOE'S NOTE ON: PERSPECTIVE

Focus too long on what's wrong and you'll miss everything that's right.

What we focus on tends to expand in our perceptions. When we focus on problems, setbacks and imperfections in our lives, careers, or relationships, we are often so absorbed by what's "going wrong" that we miss what's going well!

The more we dwell on the negative, the more our mindset gets conditioned to expect (and therefore attract) more of the same.

In relationships, this might look like fixating on your partner's quirks or occasional mistakes, while forgetting the laughter or support they consistently offer.

At work, it might mean stressing over that one failed project and ignoring the five that went fabulous.

We must rebalance our perspective. Now this doesn't mean we should ignore problems, but rather to avoid letting them blind us to the good that's happening!

Practicing Gratitude and Perspective aren't just "feel-good" exercises, they're powerful tools for staying grounded, hopeful, and resilient. Life isn't perfect, but neither is it all bad... that is, unless you convince yourself it is!

CHAPTER TWO
The Habit of Thought

Ernest Holmes, the author of The Science of Mind, said . . .

Change Your Thinking, Change Your Life...

Let's look at this "habit of thought" thing for a minute—because it's sneakier than a raccoon in your trash in the middle of the night.

We tend to think of habits as physical things. Biting our nails. Devouring a bag of chips. Hitting the snooze button nine times. But the truth is, the most powerful habits aren't the ones we can see—they're the ones running inside our heads 24/7 like a background app we didn't even know was open.

Thoughts become habits in the same way brushing your teeth did. You don't wake up and decide, "Today I shall brush my teeth." No. You do it because it's automatic. It's wired in. And that's exactly how we end up automatically thinking things like:

"This always happens to me."

"I'm not good at that."

"I could never pull that off."

"Success is for other people. Probably people who wear suits."

These thoughts weren't chosen. They were installed by well-meaning people, cultural norms, teachers, random relatives, maybe even a judgy guidance counselor—and your subconscious just nodded along and said, "I Accept These Terms and Conditions."

And boom, just like that, a thought becomes a belief. The belief becomes a pattern. The pattern becomes a personal reality. And then you're out there thinking, "Why do I keep ending up in the same spot, despite all this reading, journaling and vision boarding?"

It's because your subconscious mind is driving the car. You, my friend, are just sitting in the passenger seat, screaming affirmations out the window.

Now don't get me wrong, affirmations, vision boards, and journals are all great tools. But unless we start rewiring those deeply embedded habits of thought, all the surface work is just that—surface work. You're not lazy. You're just misguided.

What I'm going to show you in this book is a way to re-center yourself. To take those unconscious mental habits, shine a flashlight on them, and start choosing different ones. Consciously. Repeatedly. Until the new habit replaces the old one.

This isn't about hype or hustle. This is about the real, practical, human process of changing how you think so that you can finally change how you live.

Why are thoughts so powerful?

Because every action starts as a thought. Every relationship, every job, every argument, every dream, every disaster—each one was conceived in that magical brain between your ears.

The Unconscious **Authority**

Even deciding not to act is still a thought.

You think, therefore you become.

By changing the thought, and you change the outcome. Change enough outcomes, and you change your entire reality.

However, you can't simply think a new thought once and expect it to transform your life. That's like going to the gym one time and expecting a six-pack. Real change takes repetition, attention, and some discomfort. But it's also wildly empowering, because you finally get to decide who's in charge... you.

We're going to build the kind of thought habits that align with the life you actually want—not just the one you've settled into.

The next few chapters are going to show you not only how you think, but why—and most importantly, how to build thoughts that finally start working for you instead of against you.

Your Thoughts Have Power

Your thoughts are bossy little things. Think of them like sneak previews. They're basically your body's way of warming up before doing something dramatic. Ever remembered something scary and suddenly felt your heart race or your palms sweat? That's your nervous system taking your thoughts very seriously.

So, what's bouncing around in your brain most of the time? Are you even aware of what your internal playlist is broadcasting? Have you stopped to ask, "Wait... where did this thought even come from?" Have you noticed how your brain throws a little temper tantrum the second you try to think differently?

Without some mental supervision, your thoughts can piece together a wonky game plan that leads you right into habits you didn't exactly sign up for. We act the way we think—so let's make those thoughts a little more worthy.

Your Thoughts and Feelings Are Designing Your Destiny

The thoughts you have in any situation didn't just show up on their own. They're old roommates from your past, still crashing on your mental couch rent-free. And while they might be hiding under your awareness radar, you can kick them out and replace them with thoughts that serve you better.

Your subconscious mind is like rich, juicy soil. And like any soil, it doesn't care what kind of seed you toss in—it'll help it grow. Plant a weed, it'll thrive. Plant a rose or a tomato? Same deal. The soil isn't picky, it's just accommodating.

Your UA works the same way. It's that behind-the-scenes boss that pushes your thoughts—and therefore your life—in whatever direction your past trained it to believe is "normal." You can re-train the boss and plant some better mental seeds.

Your Thoughts: the Boss, Even When You're Not Aware of Them

You may be surprised to know that the thoughts that have the most impact on your life aren't necessarily the ones you're actively thinking about. They're not the deep reflections you may think they are. They're the quiet, sneaky, well-worn mental hab-

The Unconscious **Authority**

its humming along in the background. The ones that have been living in your brain since childhood.

Most of those thoughts aren't even yours.

That's right. They were installed by other people. Parents, teachers, relatives... they all contributed.

---

*A man is but the product of his thoughts . . .
what he thinks, he becomes.*

Mahatma Gandhi

Studies have found that by the age of 17, the average person has heard "No, you can't" about 150,000 times. Meanwhile, "Yes, you can" only makes about 5,000 appearances. That's a huge difference—and not exactly the pep talk you want from your inner dialog.

So what do you do when most of your self-talk sounds like a grumpy postal worker instead of a motivational speaker? Well, first, you notice it. Then you dig into where those thoughts came from. Again, they most likely weren't your idea to begin with.

I was 15, sitting at my friend's house, casually chatting with him and his brother about this big idea I had. I wanted to start my own custom painting business. I had a knack for art, and I thought, "Why not put it on wheels?" Cars, trucks, motorcycles—I was ready to airbrush some serious masterpieces.

Now, enter the peanut gallery, my friend's cute sister, who over-

Joe **Hammer**

hears us and sarcastically quips, "What are you gonna do, rob a bank?"

Did I take offense? Not really. But did her snarky comment secretly trigger my inner competitor who wanted to prove her wrong and look cool doing it? Oh, absolutely.

So a few months later, I launched the business. And to my surprise (and maybe hers), it took off fast. I was painting after school, booking jobs, and getting my designs out on the streets. It was a whirlwind—and a wildly successful one at that.

Fast forward to my sophomore year in high school. I'm in study hall one day, sketching out a new custom design for a job I had lined up later that week. Across the table sits Rick, a senior football player with ample social standing. He notices what I'm drawing and says, "That's pretty cool." For a sophomore, that was like being knighted.

But before I could bask in my moment of validation, the study hall teacher—who also just so happened to be the football coach—calls me out. "Hammer! Get up here."

I walk up, and he asks what I was doing. I explain I was just showing Rick a design he asked to see. The coach, clearly on a mission to defend the sacred silence of study hall, throws me into the hallway like I'd started a fire or something.

Rick? No punishment. Because, surprise surprise, he's on the team. Coach looks out for his players. I, on the other hand, was benched for my artistic talent.

The Unconscious **Authority**

So, I'm standing out in the hall, minding my own business and probably sulking just a little, when the school's assistant principal rounds the corner. He's a short Italian guy with an ego that could fill a stadium.

He stops, looks me over, and says, "What's the problem, Hammer?"

I tell him the story. He doesn't even pause before poking me in the chest (yes, he actually poked me) and says, "You better quit drawing pictures and get your nose in the books, or you'll never amount to anything. You need to start thinking about college if you want a real future."

And with that little ego-boosting power trip, he strutted off like he'd just solved youth delinquency.

Now, I was a relatively peaceful teen, but I was also a second-degree brown belt in Tae Kwon Do. For a brief moment, I imagined delivering a roundhouse kick so glorious it would make Bruce Lee proud. But instead, I opted for the high road.

At the time, I had no interest in college—and I was probably already making more money customizing cars and bikes than he was in his full-time job as an assistant principal. My summer that year was bonkers. The business exploded. My artwork was showing up all over town... on cars, vans, motorcycle tanks. You name it.

Then, the following year, the school librarian—who did see my potential—asked if I'd like to showcase some of my custom work in the school's main hallway. Big glass display case. Front

Joe **Hammer**

and center. You better believe I said yes.

I loaded it up with all kinds of creations: a car hood, a motorcycle gas tank, airbrushed T-shirts, a bike frame, baseball helmets—even my buddy's flamed baseball cleats. It looked like a mini art exhibit.

And somewhere in the building, that same assistant principal had to walk past it. Face-to-face with the work of the kid he said would "never make anything" of himself.

Poetic justice.

The business thrived. When I was nineteen, I signed onto a six-figure personal loan (because nothing says "I'm a grown-up now" like voluntarily going into a mountain of debt) and built a shop right on the shiny, newly expanded main highway slicing through our town. It was bold. It was terrifying. It was also one of the best decisions I ever made.

Customers rolled in like clockwork. Word spread. The demand outgrew the space faster than expected, so I expanded. Then expanded again. What started as a teenage dream and a few gallons of colorful paint turned into a full-blown, nationally recognized auto collision repair center—with a team, systems, and real adult stuff like payroll and insurance jobs.

I'm not telling you this to brag (okay, maybe just a little), but to prove a point... thoughts are powerful. Wildly powerful. But not just any thoughts—*the ones you choose to believe and act on.*

The Unconscious **Authority**

A robust desire must powerfully override a frail belief
Joe Hammer

My friend's sister and the assistant principal weren't villains. They were just people projecting their limited beliefs onto my young, blank canvas. They tried to plant seeds of doubt, and honestly, it could've worked if I hadn't already been fertilizing my brain with different thoughts—bigger ones. Bolder ones. Ones that believed I could, should, and would.

That's the thing about thoughts, they're the architects of your reality. The mental blueprints behind your behavior. And if you don't choose them intentionally, someone else will gladly hand you theirs—with no guarantee they'll lead to anything but frustration and a life that doesn't quite fit.

Thoughts create your world. Not in a fluffy, "just visualize it and manifest a mansion" kind of way, but in a boots-on-the-ground, what-you-believe-shapes-how-you-show-up kind of way.

And when your thoughts are rooted in possibility rather than fear, confidence instead of doubt—you don't just build a business. You build a life that shuts down the critics and inspires the next generation of dreamers who'd rather paint murals on vans rather than color inside the lines like everyone else.

Joe **Hammer**

The Law of Subtraction?

Contrary to what your favorite influencer might say while sipping a matcha latte and casually manifesting their dream house on Instagram, the much-hyped "Law of Attraction" isn't some magical vending machine that only spits out joy, abundance, and dream vacations. It's not Santa Claus. It's more like gravity—neutral, consistent, and completely uninterested in whether you're having a great day or an emotional meltdown.

The Law of Attraction doesn't deliver based on your hopes and vision boards; it responds to the energy surrounding your thought patterns. That energy can be bright and empowering, or cloudy and downright self-sabotaging.

Think of it like your neighborhood paperboy. He doesn't care if the news is good or bad. He just throws the paper onto your porch. Same with this law; it doesn't filter or fact-check your thoughts before delivering their results. It simply hands over the goods—whether those goods are joy, abundance, anxiety, drama, or more unpaid bills.

So, if your daily inner dialogue sounds like, "Life's hard" or "I'll never catch a break,"... congrats! You've just ordered another round of exactly that. The Law of Attraction, ever loyal, will deliver it to your mental doorstep, right on time.

On the flip side, if your thoughts are grounded in gratitude, clarity, and possibility—even just a little—it's like sending out a different kind of energy signal. One that invites growth, peace, creativity, and opportunity.

The Unconscious **Authority**

You are the one choosing those thoughts. Sometimes you're aware of it and sometimes your UA just quietly runs the show. But either way, the vibe you project becomes the reality you reflect.

Frank Outlaw said it best... "Your thoughts become your words, your words become your actions, your actions become your habits, your habits become your character, and your character becomes your destiny." It's all connected, and it all begins in that very opinionated brain of yours.

Too often, we waste time obsessing over what we don't want:

"I don't want to be broke,"
"I don't want to fail,"
"I don't want to get ghosted by a date."

And then we wonder why those things keep reappearing like reruns of a bad sitcom. The simple answer is because we're feeding them energy, even if we don't mean to.

The Law of Attraction will attract junk just as efficiently as it attracts joy. It's not just the thoughts—it's the emotional voltage behind those thoughts that activates them. You can't out-manifest your mood. If your energy is constantly bracing for disaster, don't be shocked when disaster keeps showing up.

However, you can change your thought patterns. You really can. No matter what your past looks like, no matter what beliefs you were handed as a kid, you have the power to choose again. To rewire. To rewrite the script.

And this rewiring starts with your UA—that inner voice that's been steering the ship based on old programming.

We'll be digging into exactly how to shift that in the chapters ahead. Please understand, it's not about forcing positivity. It's about recognizing the script, challenging it, and gradually replacing it with thoughts that actually serve your big, beautiful life.

The Mental Triad – Dream Team or Drama Squad?

Let's break life down real quick. Whether you're out here living your best life, building empires, or wondering how your cereal got soggy so fast—everything you experience boils down to three things. I call it *The Mental Triad*. It's simple, but don't let that fool you—it's powerful.

The three legs of the Triad are:

- You (obviously—you're the main character).

- What you think (the actual content playing in your mind).

- How you think (the tone, the vibe, the style—are you the calm, strategic type or more of a frantic squirrel energy?)

These three players are constantly shaping your reality like tiny architects building the house of your life. If your mental construction crew is working with broken tools, defective blueprints, and a playlist of doubts and complaints, don't be surprised when your "house" begins exhibiting structural issues.

Whether you're thriving, just surviving, or repeatedly tripping

The Unconscious **Authority**

over the same life lessons, your current situation is the product of this triad doing its thing. No mystery. No conspiracy theories. Just you, your thoughts, and how you're choosing to spin them.

And the Universe? Oh, it's listening. And more importantly, it's *responding*.

The Universe doesn't take sides. It doesn't have favorites. It's just over there vibing with whatever frequency you're broadcasting. You give it fear, doubt, and a steady stream of "I can't"? It says, "Cool, got it. More of that coming up." You broadcast confidence, excitement, and belief? It says, "Gotcha, let's line up some blessings."

Look, you don't have to believe in woo-woo energy fields or spiritual algorithms to get this. It's like electricity—it doesn't care what you're using it for. You can power a cozy nightlight or a medieval torture device, and electricity says, "Sure, no judgment here." Same goes for the Law of Attraction. It's not reading your moral compass—it's just reacting to your settings.

The good news is that you've got the power to shift this entire system. That challenge you're dealing with? That pattern you keep repeating? That self-sabotaging thought that creeps in? You can flip the script.

But you'll only flip it if the benefit of changing outweighs the benefit of staying stuck. Oprah Winfrey didn't build an empire because her childhood was perfect. She built it because the vision she had for her future was way louder than the echoes of her past.

So ask yourself, what thoughts are fueling your Triad? Are you operating from a place of excitement and expansion? Or are you letting fear and "what ifs" drive the bus?

Because remember, your UA, that inner autopilot you didn't even know was flying the plane... doesn't edit. It doesn't say, "Oh wait, this thought is insecure and kind of messy—let's skip it." Nope. It says, "Got it! Right away, boss!" and starts lining up people, places, and experiences to match that inner energy.

It's not out to get you. It's just extremely obedient.

So the question is, Are you ready to upgrade the crew in your Triad and rebuild the house with better materials?

The Universe is always delivering. You might as well start placing better orders!

The Power of Words (your mouth is likely working against you)

Alright, we've talked about thoughts. Now let's talk about their louder cousins, *words*.

What you speak—out loud or in that cozy, private place in your own head—isn't just noise. It's programming. Verbal code. Every word you mutter, whisper, shout, or mentally rehearse is like pressing "send" on an email to your Unconscious Authority. And it's never ignored.

The Unconscious **Authority**

Whatever your thoughts, so will be your experiences.
Joe Hammer

Whether you're speaking to a friend, your dog, or the traffic during rush hour, your words are orders to your subconscious. They're action commands. Instructions. And the UA, being the good little soldier that it is, doesn't question your orders. It doesn't pause and say, "Hmm, he's clearly having a rough day—let's ignore that whole 'I'm a failure' thing." Nope. The UA goes, "Got it, boss! Preparing to manifest more failure as requested!"

Let's be honest—how many times have you said (or heard someone say) things like:

"I'm terrible with money."

"I can't lose weight if my life depended on it."

"I suck at relationships."

"I'm not a public speaker."

"I have a horrible memory."

"I'll never get ahead in life."

Now, these aren't just words. In the world of hypnotherapy, they're called *suggestions*. And while you may think you're just venting or being "realistic," what you're actually doing is submitting a formal request to your subconscious to make sure those things stay true. Like, "Hey subconscious, could you keep me locked in this same frustrating loop forever? Thanks!"

As I've mentioned earlier, your subconscious doesn't analyze. It doesn't critique your grammar or flag your self-sabotage. It doesn't even ask for clarification. It hears your words and goes, "Right away, sir," like an obedient genie.

This is how a single throwaway comment like, "I'm just not good at math," turns into a lifetime of avoiding numbers like they're cursed objects. It's how one awkward presentation in sixth grade snowballs into "I could never speak in public" well into adulthood. That internal voice? It's narrating your life—and your UA is turning that script into reality.

Let's look at an old prank that proves just how powerful this suggestion system can be. Maybe you've heard of it. A group of coworkers decide to play a little joke on Jim from accounting. It starts with one person walking up to Jim and saying, "Hey man, you okay? You look a little pale." Innocent enough, right? Then another chimes in, "Yeah dude, you seem kinda off today. Are you coming down with something?" A third coworker later follows up with, "Seriously, you don't look good at all. Maybe you should go home and rest."

Fast forward a few hours, and guess what? Jim's halfway to the parking lot, convinced he's not well, all because a few people planted the seed. No thermometer. No symptoms. Just suggestion—and Jim's own subconscious mind doing the rest of the dirty work.

That, my friend, is the power of words.

The Unconscious **Authority**

The same principle applies to you. The most dangerous suggestions aren't the ones whispered in the office—they're the ones repeated quietly, by you, to you, all the time.

And why are they so effective? Because you've got unlimited airtime with yourself. No commercials. No fact-checkers. Just you, reinforcing a storyline that might be total BS—but feels real because you've been rerunning the same mental commercial since 1984.

Words aren't the feelings themselves—they're just the packaging. But if you say them enough, the subconscious treats them like gospel and programs the nervous system to feel and react accordingly. Boom—new emotional pattern installed, no user manual required.

So yes, words matter. A lot. They can be tools or weapons. Therapy or poison. They can build you up or quietly convince you to sit down and settle for less. Which brings us to this important life hack... start paying attention to what you say, especially when no one else is around to hear it. Because someone's always listening.

And that someone is your Unconscious Authority.

Words Influence Your Emotions

Unsolicited advice is the junk mail of human interaction. Nobody asked for it, nobody wants it, and it usually goes straight into the mental recycling bin—unless we make the mistake of opening it and letting it in.

Joe **Hammer**

Whether it's about your health, your appearance, your career, your relationship, or how you load your dishwasher—never allow someone to offer their two cents if you didn't ask for it in the first place. If someone insists on handing you an uninvited opinion wrapped in a passive-aggressive smile, simply:

Politely thank them for their "concern,"

Firmly tell them you didn't request feedback,

And kindly invite them to keep their insights where they originated—inside their own head.

Once you set that boundary, you'll be surprised how quickly people stop using your life as a dumping ground for their unprocessed thoughts.

Now, if someone does sneak in a comment before you can swat it away, don't panic. Just don't react. Don't argue. Don't spiral. Instead, take a moment, breathe, and ask yourself:

How do I truly feel about this?

Because what you feel is infinitely more important than what they think.

Anytime someone says something to you—especially something loaded, opinionated, or less-than-kind—your brain gets to work faster than a computer line of code. It starts pulling files from your mental archives, digging through past experiences related to those words. And before you know it, a whole emotional machine is triggered. Thoughts spark memories, memories stir up

The Unconscious **Authority**

emotions, and suddenly you're reliving that time in eighth grade when someone laughed at your haircut.

These reactions aren't just emotional, they're neurological and physiological. Your entire body gets involved. That's how powerful words are. And if you're not careful, you can end up reacting to the ghost of a moment from 20 years ago instead of what's actually happening in the present moment.

Let's take a simple, relatable example. You say to yourself, "Ugh, I think I'm coming down with something."

Well, guess who's listening? Your subconscious mind. And like an overachieving but slightly neurotic personal assistant, it grabs that message and starts preparing your body to be sick. This is known as an *autosuggestion*—a fancy word for when you tell your body to do something and it says, "Okay!" even if it's not in your best interest. Your nose starts tingling, your throat gets scratchy, and before you know it, you're curled up with a blanket, some chicken soup, and a decision you wish you hadn't made.

Now imagine what happens when someone else says something hurtful or critical. Your UA doesn't stop to question it. It just checks your personal history, matches the statement to past hurts or perceived slights, and triggers an emotional reaction. These connections often happen without your conscious awareness. It's not the words themselves doing the damage—it's the emotional landmines they set off.

And don't forget, the energy behind the words matters just as much. If someone calls you a "liar," your reaction may not be just about the current accusation—it might also pull up feelings from a childhood moment when you were wrongly blamed for breaking your grandma's vase. Even worse, the person calling you a liar might be projecting their own dishonesty onto you, using their words as a mirror for their unresolved shame.

Either way, *their words are not your truth.*

When that happens, your job is to pause and reflect. Not on them, but on you. Ask yourself what you know to be true. And remind yourself that the person talking doesn't know the whole you, they only know the version of you filtered through their own issues and life quirks.

Words, as harmless as they may seem, are never "just words." They're containers of meaning, emotion, and energy. Let's take the word "cancer," for example.

That one word? It's not a disease. It's just a word that describes a category of disease. But when spoken by a doctor in a white coat, it becomes gospel. Why? Because of all the weight, history, and fear we've collectively attached to it.

When you hear that word, you still have a choice in how you respond. You can let it drag you into a panic spiral fueled by thalamic-level reactions (more on that shortly), or you can take a breath, zoom out, and remind yourself: This is a suggestion. It's a professional opinion. It's not a death sentence. It's not your story. It's not you.

The Unconscious **Authority**

You can choose to respond with clarity instead of chaos.

Words are powerful—*but only if you let them be.*

And by the way, this goes both ways. You don't just need to defend yourself from others' words, you've got to be thoughtful about the ones you speak, too.

I was recently at a board meeting for a nonprofit (yes, I do serious things occasionally), and we were discussing an $1,100 annual expenditure. One board member voiced concern. Another chimed in and said, "Well, it's less than a hundred bucks a month—that's not bad."

To which the original board member snapped back, "Yes, I know. I can do the math."

Now, was that snippy reply about the math? Probably not. Did the second person mean to insult her intelligence? Definitely not. But her UA was having a field day, lighting up some old, buried moment when she probably was made to feel inferior or dismissed. The word wasn't the problem—the meaning behind the word (and the meaning her subconscious assigned to it) was.

So remember, words are vehicles for energy and suggestion.

Reactions often stem from the past, not the present. And while we can't always control what others say, we can absolutely choose what to absorb.

Be kind with your words—to others, and especially to yourself. Again, the UA is always listening.

Joe **Hammer**

The Double-Sided Excuse

There were once two men who grew up in the same tough neighborhood. They both came from poor families and faced the same struggles.

Years later, one of them became wildly successful, living the good life. The other? He struggled daily, barely getting by, living on the streets.

Both were interviewed and asked the same question: "How did you end up where you are today?"

They both gave the same answer:

"Because of my childhood."

Wait, what?

The successful man said, "I never wanted to go back to that life, so I worked my butt off to build something better."

The struggling man said, "Well, I had a rough childhood, so this is just how life turned out for me."

Same past, totally different thoughts about it. One used it as fuel. The other used it as an excuse.

That's the power of how we think about our experiences—not the experiences themselves, but the meaning we assign to them. One turned pain into purpose. The other turned pain into a permission slip to stop trying.

Next time you're out in public, do a little people-watching ex-

The Unconscious **Authority**

periment. Look at how people carry themselves. Some walk with purpose, chin up, chest out, like they're headed to close a deal or star in their own action movie. Others shuffle around like they lost their last friend and their favorite snack all in the same day.

What's the difference? They're walking through the same world... but living in very different mindsets.

The UA doesn't care who you wish you were. It operates on who you believe you are. Not your "New Year, New Me" self. Just the version of you you've been conditioned to think is real.

Had I listened to my friend's sister (who thought starting a business meant robbing a bank) or my assistant principal (whose advice came with a side of short-man complex), I might've bought into the idea that I was destined to fail.

But I didn't. And that's what matters.

We all meet "thought bullies" in life—people who try to hand you their limiting beliefs like a Las Vegas strip-club flyer you didn't ask for. And a lot of them, unfortunately, have job titles and corner offices.

You don't have to take their beliefs and make them your own. Are your thoughts building your future or excusing your present?

Joe **Hammer**

Authority Figure Curses – Wisdom Gone Wild

We've all had those run-ins with authority figures who, bless their hearts, meant well, but ended up handing us belief bombs wrapped in terrible advice. Like my mom, who once jokingly told me that eating bread crust would make my hair curly.

Then there was my assistant principal spewing his version of life wisdom. Little did he know that I didn't want to spend years getting a diploma so I could punch a timecard and make someone else rich. I had a vision. A desire to build a business now, not after 37 general ed classes and a puffy student loan.

The issue wasn't that he hated me, he probably thought he was helping. But he was filtering life advice through his lens. His programming. His beliefs. He didn't know squat about being self-employed or starting a business. Naturally, his worldview was anchored in higher education. Mine? Making money doing what I loved.

That assistant principal wasn't the only one. We've all had a rotating cast of characters influencing us before our brains were done developing. Parents, grandparents, teachers, pastors, babysitters, etc.

And while some of them meant well, like my mom, many of them don't offer advice, they pass on their fears, their doubts, their childhood hang-ups, and their outdated rulebooks... right into our wide-open, spongey little minds. Their stuff quietly became our stuff.

The Unconscious **Authority**

And just because we're all grown up now doesn't mean we're off the hook. The cast has changed, but the programming continues. Today it's your boss, your doctor, the financial guy, or that very serious-sounding news anchor warning you about five more things to panic about before bedtime.

For example, you go to a doctor who gives you a detailed game plan to manage your illness. You follow it to a T... because they're a professional, right? But someone else with the same condition skips the pills and goes to a faith healer who just taps their forehead like they're rebooting a Wi-Fi router—and boom! They're better.

What's the common denominator?

Belief.

Studies on placebos have shown that sometimes the sugar pill outperforms the actual drug—not because the pill has magic powers, but because belief does.

We have to be very cautious about whose beliefs we're adopting—especially if we assume their age, credentials, or title makes them infallible. They might wear a lab coat, carry a clipboard, or drive a BMW, but they're still humans. Humans with their own weird programming. Just like us.

That well-meaning authority figure you're listening to might be running on childhood software that has never been updated.

Sometimes that programming can be downright dangerous. History is littered with tragic examples—like the devastating cases of people who followed unstable religious leaders like Jim Jones, David Koresh, or Marshall Applewhite, all because they believed in the power of the messenger.

Your belief in someone else's authority can become a curse if it overrides your own wisdom.

You don't need to rebel against every person in a position of power, but you do need to filter their words through your own discernment. Because not all advice is good, not all titles are trustworthy, and not all bread crusts make your hair curly.

The Condescending Minister – Yeah, the Halo Slipped

I had a firsthand run-in with a "spiritual" authority figure. It happened at a spiritual center where I'd been volunteering in the marketing and communications department for years under the previous minister. All was well. Then came the new minister—bright-eyed, freshly robed, and carrying the invisible clipboard of control.

Just a few weeks into her new role, I was called into a meeting. Apparently, I hadn't replied to one of her emails fast enough. Gasp. Scandal. A spiritual offense.

She sat across from me, visibly irritated, and launched into what can only be described as a passive-aggressive PowerPoint presentation—minus the slides. After grilling me with the intensity of an IRS audit, she dropped the golden line… "You have a passive/aggressive attitude."

The Unconscious **Authority**

Excuse me?

From a minister, no less! A person who literally signs up to operate under a spiritual code of compassion, kindness, and integrity? Instead, I got condescension served with a side of self-importance and a dash of emotionally undercooked projection.

Now, I could've let that accusation crawl into my brain and set up shop. But instead, I paused. Breathed. And did the most powerful thing anyone can do in the face of nonsense... I dismissed it.

Truth was, her reaction wasn't about me. It was an overblown, disproportionate response to something as trivial as a missed email—something that happens every day to every human with an inbox. This wasn't about communication protocol. It was about power... or more specifically, a perceived lack of it.

Whether you're a minister, a magician, a mathematician or a mechanic—when you lash out at someone over something small, it's usually because you feel small. I saw her outburst for what it really was... a flashing neon sign that read, "I'm not okay in here."

And sure enough, that incident wasn't unique. Turns out, other folks had similar encounters with her not-so-spiritual approach. A few months later, she resigned from her post and took a job in an office—probably a better match for her temperament and tendency to weaponize her title.

The moral of the story?

Joe **Hammer**

Don't be dazzled by someone's title, degree, or fancy parking spot. A business card doesn't guarantee wisdom. Just because someone wears a collar, holds a gavel, or has a doctorate doesn't mean their inner world isn't a dumpster fire.

Programming trumps position. Her years of spiritual education were no match for the deep-seated beliefs and emotional habits she hadn't yet faced.

Be cautious around people in authority. Don't hand over your trust just because someone's nameplate says "Reverend," "Doctor," or "Regional Manager of Enlightenment." You were exposed to enough of that as a kid. But now you've got options.

Use discernment. Guard your mind. And when someone starts slinging spiritual guilt over a late email, do what I did... smile, walk away, and leave them to stew in their own sermon.

Authority Figures

Who were the "People of Trust" who have placed their unwanted and undesired beliefs into my mind?

Form: *Authority Figures*
Download this exercise form at www.UnconsciousAuthority.com/forms

The Unconscious Authority

The Power of Thought

When you're gifted with the power of thought
It is a wonderful thing in a way,

But it can also create problems
If your thoughts tend to go astray.

The power of thought brings things to light
That we tend to postpone

But now folks with the power of thoughts
Have today become quite known

So if you possess the power of thought
And don't know how to use it

Consult others who have the same quality,
But very seldom abuse it.

For the Lord gave us the power of thought
To do with as we choose

So hang on to it, always,
It is one power you don't want to lose!

—Norman Van Horne

JOE'S NOTE ON: ACCUSATIONS

If someone is calling you a liar out of nowhere, check their pants... odds are, they're on fire

Sometimes, people accuse you of stuff they're actually guilty of themselves. It's not about you—it's just them wrestling with their own messy conscience.

This is most often because they can't (or won't) face their own guilt, so they project it onto someone else. It's often a mirror for their unresolved shame.

The accusations are not really about you—they're about them. While accusing you, they're actually reflecting (many times unconsciously) the shame they feel inside about their own behavior that they haven't dealt with.

Understanding this helps you to not take things personally.

If someone unfairly labels you or accuses you, it might say more about what they're hiding or ashamed of than anything about your character.

Learn to see the source of the attack, not just the attack itself.

It's like a skunk blaming you for the smell...

No dude... That's YOU!

CHAPTER THREE
We Become What We Contemplate

Many people wander through life feeling like they're trapped in a loop of quiet frustration, low-grade anxiety, and that nagging sense that something's missing, but they can't quite put their finger on what. I call this phenomenon, *living a life of quiet desperation*. And most people don't even realize they're doing it.

They wake up, go through the motions, check the boxes, smile when expected, but deep down, they feel stuck. There's a heavy fog of discontent that follows them around like a moody cloud, and yet, there's no conscious awareness of how it got there or how to clear it.

Why?

Because their inner world that's running the show... their thoughts, beliefs, and self-talk goes largely unchecked. We're constantly contemplating our limitations, our worries, our fears, our failures... and guess what? The UA takes note. It doesn't judge. It just listens, accepts, and gets to work bringing more of that into our reality.

We become what we contemplate—not what we wish, not what we daydream, and definitely not what we scribble in our jour-

Joe **Hammer**

nal. *We become what we habitually think, feel, and mentally rehearse.*

Truth is, most people attempt to change their lives with surface-level intentions like New Year's resolutions, vision boards, motivational memes, etc., but they never penetrate the deeper vault of the UA, where true transformation happens. It's like planting seeds on concrete and wondering why nothing grows.

You might say, "I want a better job," or "I deserve love," or "I'm ready for abundance"—but if your UA has been spoon-fed years of evidence that says otherwise, guess what it's going to believe? That old programming still has the steering wheel, and it's not letting go just because you think about a dream vacation.

The real "Secret" isn't just saying nice words or thinking happy thoughts. That's the frosting. The real secret is getting those new beliefs and desires locked into the UA, where they can be silently and efficiently put to work behind the scenes, 24/7, without you having to consciously manage every step.

That's the inner alchemy... the part where transformation gets real. When your inner world finally matches the outer world. Your UA, once your greatest saboteur, becomes your most loyal employee—one who never complains and always follows orders. *It follows your dominant thoughts, not your wish list.*

So if you've ever wondered why you keep ending up in the same relationships, the same job rut, the same emotional patterns—don't just look at your circumstances. Look at what you've been contemplating all along.

The Unconscious **Authority**

Because that, my friend, is what you've been unconsciously becoming.

Silent Signals

Let's face it, we've all got our quirks, imbalances, and slightly weird emotional patterns. That's part of what makes us the beautiful hot messes we are. Perfection is overrated, anyway. Most of the time, we're able to keep things balanced while juggling life's lemons. But sometimes the lemons hit us in the face, and we reach for "coping mechanisms" like booze, comfort food, late-night infomercials or some unneeded crap from Amazon.

These emotional imbalances usually have roots deep in our past, hiding out in places we're not consciously aware of. They don't come with warning labels or user manuals.

Think of it like your TV. You can't see the signal flying through the air, but you can see what shows up on screen. Some channels are uplifting, like nature documentaries or baking competitions. Others are grim—like true crime marathons or political debates. The TV doesn't judge what comes through, it just plays what it's tuned into. You decide what to watch.

Your UA works the same way. It doesn't judge your thoughts. It just tunes into the ones you've spent the most time watching… especially the reruns from your past. The more you watch them, the more they show up. Even if you're dying to change the channel, it can feel like the remote's buried between the couch cushions of your subconscious.

Joe **Hammer**

So what does this look like in real life?

Easy. Just look around.

Pay attention to the people in your circle—friends, coworkers, etc. Some are energized and optimistic. Others might seem like human thunderclouds. Sometimes the people who look like they have it all together are the ones who are the crankiest. Meanwhile, folks with fewer resources or challenges somehow radiate gratitude and peace. Go figure.

Then there are those poor souls who always seem cursed. Their brand-new car is already making weird noises. Their dog runs away. Their TV explodes one day after the warranty ends. Their pool springs a leak in the middle of winter. It's like the universe has them on speed dial for bad luck.

On the flip side, you've probably seen people who seem to live in a magical vortex of good fortune. Great friends, loving relationships, endless opportunities—they just click. It's not magic. It's not luck. It's a *habit of thought* they've trained into their subconscious.

Think of your thoughts as Google search terms. If you keep searching for stuff you don't like—people, events, situations—your brain will say, "Oh! You must want more of that!" and deliver it right to your doorstep. It's called *The Reticular Activating System*. It's like your brain's personal concierge, and it's very good at what it does. Even if what it's delivering is stuff you really don't want.

The Unconscious **Authority**

Your mind has come a long way since your diaper-wearing days. Back then, it was basically a sponge—soaking up everything around it. And much like a real sponge, it wasn't picky. A sponge doesn't ask, "Excuse me, is this Evian or toilet water?"

Nope. It just absorbs whatever it touches—clean water, dirty water, mystery liquids, or even something corrosive enough to melt its little spongey insides. No judgment. Just full-on absorption.

Those who take effort to better control their mind will enjoy domination over their destiny.

Joe Hammer

Our young minds worked the same way. We absorbed ideas, beliefs, and emotional patterns from the people around us—parents, teachers, babysitters, cranky neighbors, cartoons with questionable messages—all without filtering or questioning any of it. We simply soaked it all in.

The challenge? Some of what we absorbed was great—like kindness, creativity, or confidence. But other stuff, not so much. Fear, self-doubt, limiting beliefs, weird opinions about money, success, etc.

And because our early minds didn't have a built-in "mental filter," all that programming slipped right into our subconscious without resistance. That's what's still driving many of our thoughts and reactions today.

Joe **Hammer**

The Mind's Processors — Your Brain's "Odd Couple"

There are two key processors working the mental gears in your noggin: the *Hypothalamus* and the *Cortex*. Think of them as roommates—one is the emotional hothead, the other is the chill thinker.

The hypothalamus is in charge of emotions. It's quick, impulsive, and often dramatic—like a toddler who missed nap time.

The cortex, on the other hand, handles logic and thought. It's the responsible roommate who actually reads the lease before signing it.

The hypothalamus gets first dibs on reacting to life's curveballs. Yep, emotions cut the line. The cortex? Always second in command, patiently sipping coffee and waiting to be asked for its opinion.

Here's how they usually show up in a situation:

THALAMUS:	CORTEX:
Panic	Questions
Anxiety	Observations
Fears	Reflections

So when you get bad news, stub your toe, or your latte comes out with whole milk instead of almond, your emotional processor is already sounding the alarm before your cortex can even say, "Hmm, let's think this through."

That's why you've probably heard the advice, "Count to ten before reacting." It's not just to avoid launching into a monologue of rage—it's to give your cortex time to catch up and say, "Maybe we don't need to throw things quite yet."

Want to see a thalamic (emotion-first) response in action? Watch animals or toddlers... A mountain lion sees a rabbit. BAM! No hesitation. Dinner is served. Take a toy from a toddler. Cue the meltdown. Instant tears.

Neither paused to think it over. They didn't check the pros and cons or file a report. They just reacted. And while we might not pounce on rabbits or throw tantrums in the cereal aisle, we still experience those gut-level responses on a daily basis... sometimes without even realizing it.

Repeated emotional reactions release stress chemicals in the body. Over time, these little hormone bombs can affect everything from your weight to your relationships, even your health. It's like your cells are attending a drama class, and they're getting really good at panic, fear, and anxiety.

So what can you do?

Simple. Build the habit of *awareness*. Start noticing your snap reactions. Ask your partner or friends to gently call you out when you overreact. And above all, train yourself to respond, not react.

Responding means you:

- Question instead of panic.
- Observe instead of spiral.
- Reflect instead of rage.

Just let your cortex take the wheel more often. Count to 10, breathe, and be the calm in the emotional hurricane.

Never become the emotion. Observe it like a nosy neighbor. It's passing through, not moving in.

It's Time for You to Be Sick

Remember the story I shared about the office worker who came down with the sniffles right after someone suggested he looked under the weather? That wasn't just a coincidence, it was a textbook case of mind-over-mucus.

Turns out, we humans are weirdly suggestible. If someone sneezes within a five-foot radius of us during "cold and flu season" (which, by the way, is a marketing term, not a medical one), we suddenly start sniffing, sneezing, and Googling symptoms we definitely didn't have two minutes ago. Why? Because the UA takes the idea of illness and runs with it.

Studies have shown that emotionally-based symptoms—like those caused by stress, anxiety, frustration, and worry—can actually trigger real, measurable changes in the body. And if you're exposed to enough "suggestions" of illness (flu commercials), your body might just decide it's time to say yes to that sinus infection.

There's a phenomenon called *somatization*, and it's when emotional or mental distress doesn't just hang out in your mind—it manifests in your body. That headache? It's your unresolved stress screaming for attention. That persistent stomach issue? It

The Unconscious **Authority**

might be less about your lunch and more about your lingering anxiety.

People who experience somatoform disorders don't just think they're sick. They are sick—because their symptoms are real. There's often no physical cause doctors can find. But try telling that to someone who's actually doubled over in pain—they'll look at you like you're crazy.

Your body and mind are so deeply connected. They'll play out a whole performance based on nothing but an emotional script. Your UA, being the eager overachiever that it is, will conjure physical symptoms as if your organs are part of a live theater production. "Now starring... Heartburn, brought to you by unresolved guilt!"

So yes, while your immune system is certainly a powerhouse, your beliefs, fears, and emotional patterns may just be the true scriptwriters behind the scenes.

Bottom line? You might not be able to think your way into a six-pack abs, but you can think your way into a sick day. Which is a pretty compelling reason to start being more mindful about what you allow into your headspace—because your body is always listening.

And sometimes... it's got terrible taste in programming.

Joe **Hammer**

Thalamic & Cortex Responses

What are some of the things that "push your buttons? (*Thalamic response*)

What would be a better, less energized response to those situations? (*Cortex response*)

Form: *Thalamic & Cortex Responses*
Download this exercise form at www.UnconsciousAuthority.com/forms

Change the Channel

Your mind's got more channels than cable—and some of them are pure drama.

Picture this: You're chilling on the couch after a long day, remote in hand, just looking for something light to watch. You flip to a channel and bam!... it's a horror movie already halfway through. Blood, creepy music, a doll that needs an exorcism...

Nope. Not today, Satan. What do you do?

You change the channel.

With one simple click, you dodge the terror, the tension, and the nightmares that would've followed you into your nighttime dreams. Did the movie disappear from the universe? Of course not. It's still running in the background, screaming at someone

The Unconscious **Authority**

else. But you aren't watching it anymore because you took control of the remote. You protected your peace.

This isn't about Netflix. It's about your mind.

Your UA is always "on," always absorbing input, whether it's a sitcom or a nagging vibe from a friend who thrives on drama. And just like your TV, your mind doesn't judge the content. It doesn't ask, "Is this good for me?" It just absorbs whatever it's tuned to.

So what happens when you're stuck in a conversation with a person who only speaks in doom and gloom? When every sentence they utter feels like a trailer for an emotional disaster film?

You guessed it... *change the channel.*

Switch your internal dial. Don't feed your UA the horror film of their negativity. Tune in to a better frequency... one filled with positivity, hope, humor, and positive people.

Fact is, the thoughts you let in, the people you surround yourself with, the media you consume... all of it is programming your subconscious mind. If you're constantly tuned into toxic chatter, you start running toxic thought reruns 24/7. But if you start intentionally flipping to channels filled with inspiration, gratitude, growth, and love, you begin to rewire your inner world.

You wouldn't voluntarily watch a movie that gives you nightmares, right? So why sit through conversations or environments

Joe **Hammer**

that fill your mental DVR with doubt, fear, or shame?

Grab the remote. Own the click. And when in doubt? Go find the mental channel with puppies, stand-up comedy, or someone reminding you that you're capable of amazing things.

Welcome to better programming.

Kites and Anchors

Whose lifting you up and who is holding you hostage?

Let's talk metaphors. Big, breezy metaphors. On one hand, you've got kites—colorful, soaring, playful things that dance in the sky. And on the other hand? You've got anchors—heavy, rusted hunks of metal that don't move unless the ship's captain brings it to the surface.

An anchor is made to hold something in place. Its sole job is to keep things exactly where they are, no matter how strong the current or how exciting the adventure waiting just beyond the horizon. Reliable? Sure. But also aggressively resistant to change. Anchors are not here for growth. They're here for immobility. And a whole lot of it.

A kite, on the other hand, is a thing of wonder. It's light, agile, responsive. It's still tethered and grounded, just like us, but it

The Unconscious **Authority**

plays with the wind, shifts directions with ease, and uses the very force that could destroy it as the thing that helps it soar. Kites don't resist the wind. They rise with it.

You've got both kites and anchors in your life, and sometimes if you're being honest, you might even be one or the other.

Kite people are your hype squad. They uplift you, fuel you with encouragement, and clap when you win—even if they're not winning themselves. They want to see you fly. They aren't threatened by your glow. They cheer it on. These are the friends who say, "I see what you're doing—and I love it for you." They may not be on the same flight path, but they'll help you catch wind.

Anchor people, though? Whole different story. Anchors hate movement. They resent growth. If you start rising, they start panicking. They want you safe; their version of safe. Which usually means stuck in the same emotional zip code they've been living in since 1987. They'll pull your metaphorical chain, drip sarcasm into your dreams, and mutter "must be nice" when you share your goals. And honestly? Most of them don't even know they're doing it. Their UA is stuck in anchor mode, running a program written by fear, failure, or family folklore.

You can't make an anchor into a kite. Not unless they want to become one. And even then, they'll need to rewrite some deep internal programming... and maybe get a little therapy, a little sunlight, and a whole new script. That's their work, not yours.

So what can you do? You can choose who holds your string. You

Joe **Hammer**

can decide how long you let that anchor dig into your soul before you snip the cord and go full kite mode.

And what if the anchor is your spouse? Your dad? Your lifelong bestie who now thinks manifesting is "a cult" and dreams are "pies in the sky?"

It's tricky. But it's still your responsibility to manage your energy. If cutting ties feels too extreme, set boundaries. Tell your loved ones, "Unless what you're about to say has a chance of sending me airborne, I'm not available for it." You don't owe anyone a front-row seat to your life if they're there to cast shadows on your dreams.

And if you've realized you've been the anchor? I have good news for you. This book is your ticket to becoming a kite again. We've got string, wind, and all the encouragement you'll need.

Just remember, the sky has more room than the harbor. And it comes with better views. Choose who you fly with—and never apologize for letting go of what keeps you from taking off.

Surround yourself with those who voice more gratitudes than grumbles.

Richelle E. Goodrich

The Unconscious **Authority**

Kites & Anchors

Kites

Who are the kites in my life?

What I can do to better embrace these kites in my life:

Anchors

Who are the anchors in my life?

What I can do to avoid or reduce these anchors' influences in my life?

Form: *Kites & Anchors*
Download this exercise form at www.UnconsciousAuthority.com/forms

Cheerleaders and Coaches

Similar to kits and anchors, we have Cheerleaders and Coaches. Our ego craves affirmation—especially in moments of uncertainty or insecurity. And who better to turn to than our closest friends? Our cheerleaders. They love us, believe in us, and genuinely want us to succeed. But their support, however heartfelt, often lacks the objectivity or expertise we truly need.

The ego doesn't seek correction—it seeks confirmation. It looks for validation that says, "You're on the right track," even when that track leads nowhere helpful. That's why we often rely on the wrong people for advice. Not because they're unkind or ill-intentioned, but because they're more inclined to reinforce our current choices than challenge them. Cheerleaders offer emotional comfort, but comfort is not the same as clarity.

Imagine a sports team where the cheerleaders run the playbook. There'd be nonstop applause and high energy—but no direction, no adjustments, and ultimately, no wins. Just enthusiastic chaos. That's exactly what happens when we try to navigate life with hype instead of strategic feedback. Encouragement without direction doesn't just stall growth—it can actually inrease dysfunction.

That's where Coaches come in. A great coach doesn't just offer praise—they provide perspective. They hold you accountable, shine light on blind spots, and help sharpen your execution. Coaches care less about your comfort in the moment and more about your long-term outcome. They don't flatter your ego, they challenge your thinking. And the truth is, great coaching often feels uncomfortable—*because growth usually does.*

It's essential to recognize the difference between those who support your feelings and those who strengthen your direction. The people who elevate your life are rarely the loudest cheerleaders. They're the ones asking tough questions, offering honest feedback, and holding you to your highest potential. Cheerleaders help you feel good; coaches help you see clearly.

So when you're stuck, spinning your wheels, or chasing something uncertain, ask yourself, Am I seeking validation or direction? One soothes the ego. The other transforms your life.

The Unconscious **Authority**

Power and Will

When most people hear the word power, they imagine someone in a suit barking orders from a corner office, or a world leader speaking into a handful of microphones. Power often gets mistaken for dominance, something we wield over others. But real power doesn't shout. It doesn't puff its chest. It doesn't need a throne. Because real power is internal. You don't need a superhero cape, just clarity and conviction.

Your true power is personal. It's yours and yours alone. It's the quiet current running beneath everything you do and everything you are. And it's limitless.

Think of it like the ocean. deep, steady, vast beyond comprehension. Whether you scoop a glass or drain ten tanker trucks from it, the ocean doesn't flinch. It doesn't panic. It doesn't say, "Hey, stop taking my water." It knows. It knows that it is abundant. It knows that there's always more where that came from.

That's your inner power. An inexhaustible force, waiting for you to recognize it, tap into it, and—most importantly—trust it.

However, *you've got to claim it.*

Nobody can assign it to you. There's no badge, no ceremonial sword, no wand that gets waved and suddenly you become powerful. It's an inside job. And it starts with will.

Will is the ignition key. It's the spark that sets the whole system in motion. Your will is what turns a vague desire into a nonnegotiable decision. It's what separates the wishful thinkers from the unstoppable doers.

You've heard the stories about immigrants arriving with nothing but hope in their back pocket, working tirelessly to build lives of success, while the kids who grew up next door with all the resources in the world drift aimlessly. Why? Because the difference isn't money. It's not privilege. It's will.

Those who succeed don't just hustle, they believe. They imagine something greater, and they refuse to let that image fade. They burn it into their minds. They infuse it with emotion. They daydream about their future with the same intensity most people reserve for their next vacation. And that's the secret sauce.

Thoughts are blueprints. And when you attach emotion to those blueprints, when you infuse them with fire and vision and clarity—that's when your subconscious mind kicks in like a determined architect with no off switch.

Decide what you want. Not "more money" or "better relationships"—get precise. How much? With who? Where? When? What does it smell like? Taste like? Feel like?

Visualize it. See it play out like your favorite movie scene.

Feel it. Really feel it. The excitement, the gratitude, the joy—anchor it to your emotional body.

Repeat. Daily. Obsessively. With the same energy you'd tell everyone about your dream trip to Bora Bora.

Your UA loves specifics. It's a sucker for imagination. And once

The Unconscious **Authority**

it's dialed in, it'll start moving mountains in the background—rerouting opportunities, changing habits, tweaking perceptions... all in service of that deeply held desire.

Power lives in you. Will activates it. Emotion directs it. And belief keeps it alive.

Harness Your Imagination

Your imagination is your brain's Super Power.

Imagination isn't just child's play or daydreaming in math class. It's not just for artists or inventors or those eccentric folks. Imagination is your most important mental instrument. It's your internal architect, designer, dreamer, and director, all rolled into one. And your UA absolutely lives for imagination!

Every great invention, every brilliant idea, every piece of art, and every life-altering decision that's ever existed started the same way... as a simple thought. A mental picture. A whisper of possibility. Imagination is the bridge between what is and what could be.

Think about it. Planes, lightbulbs, the iPhone, indoor plumbing (bless that one!)... none of these just fell out of the sky. They were dreamed up first. Crafted in the mind before they ever took shape in reality.

And then there's Walt Disney. He didn't just build a theme park. He built a world—complete with singing mice, floating teacups, and trash cans that talk back to you. That's the power of imagination infused into every inch of reality. Even the trash bins were invited to the party!

You're already using your imagination... all the time. When you worry about something going wrong? When you replay an awkward conversation from three years ago? When you anticipate every worst-case scenario before breakfast? Yep. That's imagination. Just being used unconsciously—and a bit dramatically.

The goal is to harness it. To consciously take the reins and steer that wildly powerful horse of possibility in a direction that benefits you.

And just like a muscle, the more you train it, the stronger and more agile it becomes.

Inside a single lemon seed is a massive tree capable of producing thousands of lemons over decades. That's not exaggeration—that's nature. And just like that lemon seed, you have immense potential coded within you. Talents, dreams, ideas, creativity, brilliance... it's all in there. Waiting.

But like the lemon seed, it needs the right environment. It needs sunlight, water, attention, and belief. And guess what your personal fertilizer is? Imagination. Your vivid, emotional, fully-engaged imagination is the nourishment your potential craves.

Ready to Work That Brain Muscle?

Here are some tools and mindset shifts to turn your imagination from a dusty attic into a creative command center:

The Unconscious **Authority**

1. Recognize the Good

Start seeing the silver lining—not in a forced way, but in a genuinely curious, "what might be right about this?" kind of way. Train your mind to look for what's useful. When you do that, your UA goes, "Oh! We're in growth mode now," and starts serving you better options. Negative thoughts? Stop rehearsing them. They're not auditions for your future. Instead, rehearse possibility.

2. Get Organized

Let's not underestimate the power of a tidy space. Your external environment is a direct mirror of your internal state. Chaos around you? Then there's likely some chaos within you, too. Declutter. Sort. Tidy up. Then marvel at how much more clearly your imagination flows when it's not trying to break through piles of laundry and unopened mail. Nature is organized. Planets don't zigzag. Trees don't toss their branches around in confusion. Emulate nature.

3. Meditate (or at least chill the heck out)

Your mind is a tree full of noisy monkeys—thoughts jumping from branch to branch, hooting about your to-do list, your past mistakes, and whether you left the stove on. Meditation helps you gently coax those monkeys back to calm. Fifteen minutes a day. No chanting required. Just stillness. Watch what happens when your thoughts stop sprinting and start strolling.

4. Be Patient

Like a tomato plant, your dreams need consistent, daily watering. You can't dump a month's worth of water on a tomato seed in one afternoon and expect a tomato the next day. Your imagination needs daily fuel... repetition, emotion, vision. This is why motivational talks lose their magic after a few days, it's like pouring all the water on at once. You've got to drip feed belief into your brain.

5. Avoid Low Energy People and Activities

Seriously, stop letting chickens convince you that flying is dangerous. Low-energy people will drain your spark faster than a leaky battery in a flashlight. Find your kites. Stick with the eagles. Surround yourself with imagination-friendly humans. Your dreams need wind, not anchors.

6. Turn Off the Television (okay, sometimes)

TV is fine in moderation. But if your screen time is 90% murder documentaries and 10% crying at commercials, maybe rethink your media diet. Input determines output. Watch shows that inspire, that educate, that make you laugh. Your UA eats what you feed it, so don't make it live on crime dramas and chaos.

Imagination is not a luxury. It's not optional. It's not a cute little hobby. It's the first step to creating the life you actually want. Use it. Play with it. Respect it. Make it your daily companion.

The Unconscious **Authority**

You're not just a dreamer. You're a designer. You're a builder. And your mind? It's the blueprint shop of the gods.

Now go sketch out your future. Vividly. Boldly. And with a little sparkle!

Imagination!

How can I better use my imagination to visualize and internalize what I truly desire in my life?

Form: *Imagination*
Download this exercise form at www.UnconsciousAuthority.com/forms

Divine Intelligence

When I talk about Divine Intelligence, I'm not trying to recruit you into a religion, hand you a crystal, or get you to start chanting in Sanskrit. This isn't "woo-woo." It's truth.

You are a living, breathing, walking-talking extension of Divine Intelligence—call it God, Source, Universe, Consciousness, Bob... whatever makes you feel less like you're about to get smacked with a Bible. The name doesn't matter. The connection does.

Joe **Hammer**

And know this... You've never been disconnected.

That little voice in your head that says you're separate, unworthy, broken, or just "not one of those chosen people"? That voice is lying. It's been lying for years. The only real separation between you and your innate power, joy, clarity, and abundance is the belief that you're separate.

The only thing that can separate you from Divine Intelligence is your *belief* that you are separate.

That's it. Not your bad decisions. Not your credit score. Not even that time you lied about liking your friend's apple pie.

Want to know where heaven and hell actually live? Inside your mind. Right between the worry and the daydreaming.

John Milton nailed it when he wrote: "The mind is its own place and in itself can make a heaven of hell or a hell of heaven."

And if you've ever had a great day ruined by one bad thought—or a terrible day made better by a funny memory—you know it's true. Your mind is an extremely creative landscape builder. And the way it decorates that landscape?

You are not your thoughts, by the way. You are the thinker behind those thoughts. And that thinker (you) are plugged into the same Divine Wi-Fi as every enlightened sage, poet, artist and philosopher before you. Your "limitations" are mostly fiction.

Those things you think are holding you back? The "I'm not good enough," "I'm too old," "I missed my chance," "I'm not spiritual

The Unconscious **Authority**

enough," or "I don't know where to begin" things? All of them? Illusions. Fancy costumes worn by outdated programming.

Behaviors are the Manifestations of our Life Experiences.
Joe Hammer

In my work with clients, especially in regression-to-cause therapy, it becomes crystal clear... the frustrations, doubts, and emotional walls we experience today are usually the ripple effects of beliefs we adopted long ago. Beliefs we never questioned. Beliefs that were never ours to begin with.

But now, with awareness you can start dismantling those limitations like a magician revealing the secret behind the illusion.

You weren't tossed here by accident. You're not some trial run in the grand experiment of consciousness. You are, right now in this moment, perfectly equipped with everything you need to live a life of peace, joy, health, love, and purpose.

Why? Because you were built that way. You were built from the same blueprint as the oceans, the galaxies, the wildflowers, and the miracle of a rainstorm.

You came factory-loaded with potential. The update you need? It's not external. It's belief. Belief in the truth that you are not separate from Divine Intelligence. You are Divine Intelligence, having a human experience.

So take a breath. Feel that? That aliveness? That quiet, steady hum beneath the chaos of your day? That's Divine Intelligence, my friend. And it's not out there somewhere, waiting for you to earn your way to it. It's been here. In you. Always.

Your only job is to remember. Then live like it's true.

Because it is.

Let's talk real talk, making you the Jedi of your own destiny. It's time to stop thinking about your dreams, and start writing them. Yes, with actual ink. On actual paper.

This isn't your high school "goal-setting worksheet" where you scribbled things like "Get good grades" and "Work out... someday." This is you taking the steering wheel of your life with both hands, snapping on your emotional seatbelt, and telling the Universe...

"Hey, I'm ready now. Let's roll."

Writing it down is magic. No exaggeration. You're converting raw, messy, abstract desire energy into something tangible and real. You're declaring, "I'm serious about this." And the Universe loves bold declarations. It's basically the FedEx of manifestation, it just needs a clearly addressed label to know where to deliver!

Setting goals is the first step in turning the invisible into the visible.
Tony Robbins

Get Uncomfortably Specific

Now, I want you to get uncomfortably specific about what you want. Forget vague goals like "more money" or "better relationships." That's like walking into a restaurant and saying,

"Yes, I'll have food." No. Otherwise you may end up with the cold mystery soup."

Instead, I want you to write it like you're describing your ideal life to a world-class director who's about to cast you in a starring role:

- What does it look like?
- What does it feel like?
- What does it sound like?

What are you wearing? Be honest. Is it stretchy yoga pants or a crisp tailored blazer?

Who's there with you, and what are they saying that makes your heart burst into happiness?

If it's about a relationship, describe the scene like you're writing a movie script... What are you doing together? What are they saying that finally makes you feel seen and safe and appreciated?

Money Mindset: Channeling Your Inner Wealthy Weirdo

Thinking about money? Good. Let's expand your financial fantasy—but don't get weird and jump straight to "I want to be an

Joe **Hammer**

astronaut and travel to Mars." We're not trying to impress Elon Musk here.

Start by writing down what your life really looks like when you have more than enough. Enough for comfort, generosity, freedom, maybe a few guilt-free splurges. How does it feel to pay every bill on time—early, even? To log into your bank account and see extra zeroes?

Let yourself feel that emotional security. The calm. The satisfaction. The soft exhale that says, "I got this." That feeling? That's the real wealth. And guess what? It already exists in you. You're just letting it out now!

Remember when you were five and could turn a cardboard box into a spaceship with a laser cannon? Yeah. That wasn't imagination. That was genius. And you still have it. You've just let adulting get in the way.

Well, not anymore. This is your official permission slip to unleash your inner child-creator-genius-visionary. Engage all your senses. If you want that beachside villa, don't just say "beach villa"—I want the smell of the ocean in your nose, the sound of the waves in your ears, the warm teak wood under your bare feet as you sip your passionfruit smoothie and nod sagely at how far you've come.

Yes. *That* level of imagination. You're not just dreaming it. You're pre-living it. Don't let your inner skeptic run the show.

You know that voice in your head that scoffs and says,

The Unconscious **Authority**

"This is dumb." "It'll never happen." "What are you, some kind of vision board junkie now?" Yeah. That voice.

It this book's introduction, you've already provided a general overview of your desired changes. However, it's now time to drill down into the *meaningful specifics...*

Ink it like you mean it! Because when you write your life with clarity and feeling, you're not just imagining a better world... *You're building one.*

Download the **Igniting All Senses** worksheet and get to work!

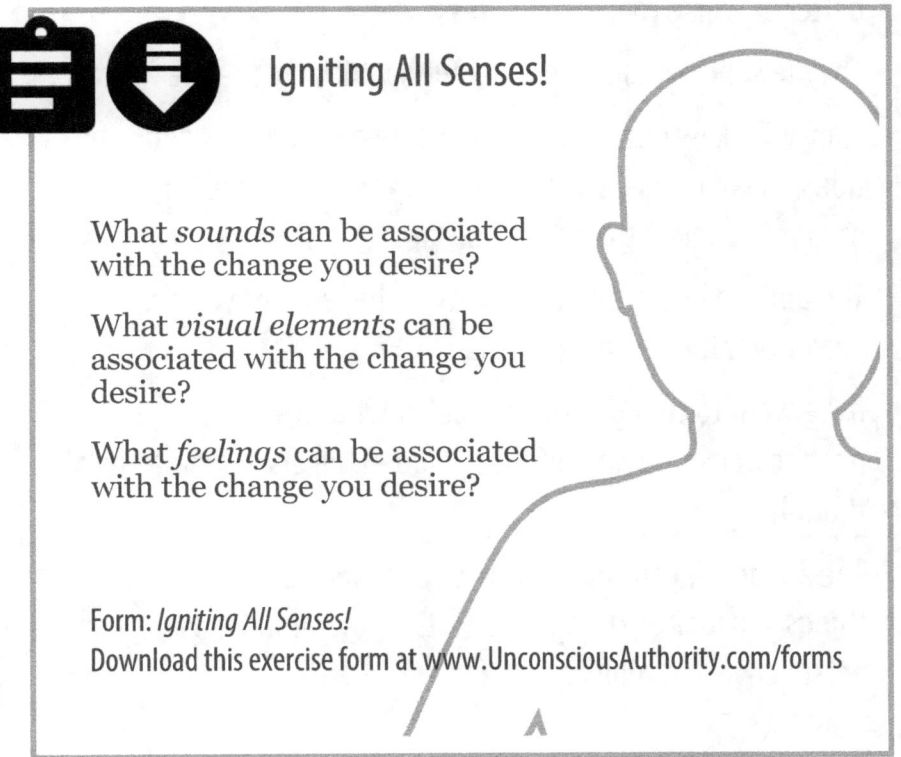

Igniting All Senses!

What *sounds* can be associated with the change you desire?

What *visual elements* can be associated with the change you desire?

What *feelings* can be associated with the change you desire?

Form: *Igniting All Senses!*
Download this exercise form at www.UnconsciousAuthority.com/forms

JOE'S NOTE ON: PERCEPTIONS

The grass only looks greener because you slipped on tinted glasses. Reality didn't change, your perception did

It's human tendency to think our lives would be better if we had a different job, relationship, house, partner, etc.

It's our perception that changed.

Our mind is filtering what we see based on beliefs, past experiences, or emotional states... which can make something seem better or worse than it actually is.

They're subconscious filters through which we see the world.

They will skew our interpretation of events, people, and situations, making things appear more appealing, more threatening, or more hopeless than they truly are.

The bottom line is that our reality is shaped more by our perception than by actual facts.

If we want to change how we feel or what we experience, we need to become aware of those hidden beliefs and patterns of thought.

The adage, "If you change the way you look at things, the things you look at change," reflects a powerful philosophy on perspective and mindset.

CHAPTER FOUR
The Technology of the Mind

Okay, so by now you may or may not fully grasp everything I've said about your habits and thoughts. If you do, gold star for you! We're about to take a deeper dive into the magnificent mystery that is your brain.

Now, once you finish this chapter, you may feel a strange and sudden urge to re-read the earlier chapters. That's not just your imagination—that's your brain starting to connect the dots. Don't fight it. Go ahead and reread to get a firm grip of the concepts. You'll notice things that didn't land before suddenly make a lot more sense, (kind of like those Star Wars movies).

The human mind is a three-part system. Think of it like a psychological smoothie made with three key ingredients. *The Conscious Mind, The Subconscious Mind* (home of the Unconscious Authority, and *The Critical Faculty*. Each part plays a vital role in how we process information, make decisions, repeat behaviors, and get in our own way with alarming consistency.

To help you visualize this trio, I've created what I like to call *The Mindberg*. Much like an iceberg, the majority of it is below the surface, which can be both fascinating as well as mildly terrifying.

Joe **Hammer**

The little tip you see above water? That's your *conscious awareness,* the part you think is running the show, however it's not. The much bigger chunk hiding underwater is your *subconscious,* quietly running all your automatic programs—your beliefs, habits, emotional responses... you know, like that weird thing you do with your eyebrows when you're lying.

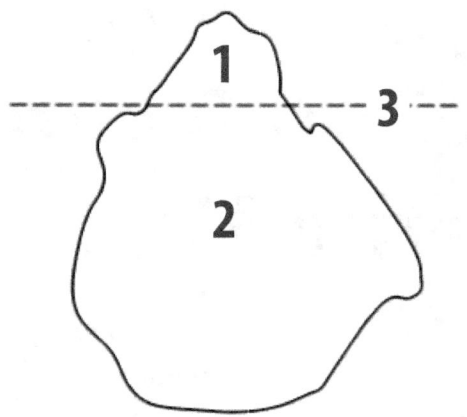

1– Conscious Mind
2– Subconscious Mind
3– Critical Faculty

Squeezed right between the two is *The Critical Faculty,* the mental gatekeeper. Its job is to screen new information like a boastful TSA agent. If something doesn't match what you already believe, it often gets rejected—many times even if it's true. This is why telling someone "you're amazing and worthy of love" can bounce off, while "you messed up again" gets escorted straight into the VIP lounge of the subconscious without question.

So now that we've met the players, let's break down how they work together (or sometimes against each other) in shaping your daily life and, more importantly, how we can work with them instead of getting emotionally mugged by their behaviors.

The Unconscious **Authority**

The Conscious Mind

Let's start with the most famous of our mental presence: *The Conscious Mind*. Now, before you get excited, understand this thing's got the smallest role in terms of its processing power. Take another look at "The Mindberg" illustration. Notice how tiny the conscious mind is compared to the vast underworld of the subconscious? Yeah. It's the tip of the iceberg. And just like the Titanic learned, it's not the visible part that'll sink the ship.

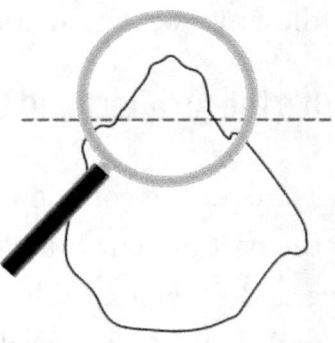

The conscious mind makes up less than 12% of your mind's total capacity. Yet for some reason, we love to act like it's in charge. It's the part that handles your outward personality... how you present in life, what you say, the polite chuckles you give at your friend's weird jokes. But in terms of real control? Not much.

You might be thinking, "Well, no wonder I have such weird friends—they're only using 12% of their mind!" Cute. But don't start polishing your Nobel Prize just yet—you're in the same 12%-powered boat, Captain.

We're often told to "be conscious" of our actions, our words, our choices. But your conscious mind doesn't have the real juice to drive meaningful, lasting change. That job belongs to its much more powerful, behind-the-scenes sibling—the subconscious. More on that powerhouse shortly. But first, let's explore what the conscious mind is good at.

It's the Architect and the Supervisor

Think of the conscious mind as the architect of your ideas. It's the part of your brain that draws up the blueprints, dreams up grand schemes, and debates whether you really need that second donut. It's logical, analytical, and loves making pro-and-con lists that you'll ignore later anyway.

It processes what's happening in the moment. If the subconscious is the CEO running the company from the shadows, the conscious mind is the overly-enthusiastic assistant manager making announcements over the intercom. It observes, it reacts, and it thinks it's calling the shots.

It Has Low Bandwidth (and no storage)

Your conscious mind may be many things—analytical, alert, obsessed with to-do lists—but one thing it's not is high capacity. In fact, it has no working memory to speak of. It's like an old-school computer with barely enough RAM to open one tab at a time. It can only focus on a single thought or task in any given moment. That's it.

Let's break it down with a quick example.

Little Billy falls and skins his knee. He wails like he's been shot. But then, Mom swoops in, gives him a hug, and gently says,

The Unconscious **Authority**

"Look at the cute kitten over by the tree." Boom—instant mood shift. Billy's brain drops the "I'm in pain!" tab and opens a new one: "I must pet that fluffy kitten." The tears stop. The knee is forgotten. Billy is now on a feline mission.

That's the conscious mind in action. It can switch attention quickly, but it can't hold multiple thoughts or emotions at once. Multitasking is a total myth at the conscious level.

Your conscious mind is always scanning, sorting, and reacting to the world through your senses, sight, sound, smell, taste, touch, and feelings. It's the watchtower of your waking state—alert and on duty, deciding what's worth noticing and what's just background noise.

And here's where things get interesting... *it doesn't make those decisions alone.*

Once your conscious mind collects the sensory data, it hands it off to that mental bouncer, *The Critical Faculty*. This guy compares the incoming info against your stored experiences, beliefs, and past programming. It then quickly decides whether to keep the thought, toss it, challenge it, or simply believe it.

(We'll get better acquainted with this mental bouncer later in this chapter.)

The bottom line is when you're consciously aware of what you're doing, you're using your conscious mind.

But don't expect it to remember much, or juggle more than one thing. That's above its pay grade.

Joe **Hammer**

It is Analytical

The conscious mind fancies itself as the brain's resident problem-solver. It's rational, analytical, and oh-so-critical. It's the Sherlock Holmes of your mental trio. It spends its time dissecting, comparing, evaluating, and attempting to draw logical conclusions. If there's a pro/con list to be made or a "should I or shouldn't I" scenario to overthink, the conscious mind is already there with a clipboard.

But, again, it doesn't have much storage space. It's basically working off sticky notes and whatever just came in five minutes ago. So while it might sound impressive that your conscious mind is calling the shots, it's really just reacting to whatever is right in front of it. It's a master of in-the-moment decisions, not long-term strategy.

The conscious mind doesn't retain long-term memory or deeply held beliefs. It's only operating on what it sees, hears, feels, or thinks *right now*.

So when you're making a snap decision, like choosing between salad or fries, it's your conscious mind weighing the options—calories versus cravings, guilt versus glory. But it's basing that decision entirely on current input and impulse, with very little understanding of your bigger behavioral patterns or emotional history.

In short, the conscious mind is the analyst—not the archive. And that, my friend, is why we'll need to dig deeper.

The Unconscious **Authority**

It is a Reason Fabricator

The conscious mind always desires to solve. It's like that over-eager coworker who jumps in with an answer before fully understanding the question. Because it's rational by nature, it needs a "reason" for every decision and action, however it doesn't care if that reason is factually accurate, emotionally true, or even remotely logical. It just wants a story that sticks. The problem? *Many of those stories are total fiction.*

Take smokers, for example. I'm sure you've heard one say, "I smoke to relax." Now, let's pause and use our actual rational mind for a second. Nicotine is a stimulant. You can't pump a stimulant into your system and simultaneously claim to be winding down. That's like saying, "I drink espresso to help me nap." Doesn't work.

But the smoker believes it. Why? Because their conscious mind has accepted it as a viable excuse. Other smokers say it. The body craves the chemical. And the ritual of the cigarette—the break, the breath, the moment away from the chaos—gets wrongly credited to the cigarette itself. The actual relief only comes later, when the addiction cycle is broken, and the body isn't twitching for its next hit. But the conscious mind has already fabricated the reason.

I once met a woman proudly flaunting her brand-new, four-thousand-dollar purse. When I asked what made her drop that kind of cash on a handbag, she said, "Oh, it's very well made. It's from Italy."

Joe Hammer

Right. And I buy $28 popcorn at the movies because it's made from higher grade kernels.

Let's be honest—she didn't buy the bag for the stitching. She bought it for the prestige, the label, and the hit of self-worth it gave her.

But the conscious mind rarely admits emotional motivation. Instead, it scrambles to find a rational justification—one it can say out loud without blushing. That's why marketing works so well. We don't buy products, we buy feelings, wrapped in a story our conscious mind can repeat at dinner parties.

This is what I call *marketing hypnosis*. The ad tells you, "You're not just buying a car—you're buying freedom." Or power. Or sex appeal. And the conscious mind goes, "Great! Freedom! Sounds reasonable. Let's do it." Meanwhile, your subconscious is the one pulling the strings, and the conscious mind is just there to provide the press release.

The conscious mind wants reasons. If it can't find one, it *invents* one. And it doesn't even know it's doing it. That's not logic—it's rationalized illusion.

So next time you catch yourself justifying a questionable decision, pause and ask, Is this the truth... or is my conscious mind just making weird excuses?

The Unconscious **Authority**

It's the Home of Our Willpower

The conscious mind is also the residence of willpower—that over-rated little force we all love to rally behind when we're about to break a bad habit, start a new routine, or resist eating that left-over cheesecake at 2 am.

But here's the thing, willpower is not built for endurance. It's more like the booster rockets on a space shuttle. Impressive? Yes. Loud and fiery? Absolutely. But their job is short-lived—they're just meant to get the rocket off the ground. Once the shuttle hits the edge of the atmosphere, those rockets fall away and the real engine—the deep, internal power source—takes over.

Willpower helps you launch. It gives you the initial push when you decide to wake up early, quit smoking, eat kale, or start meditating. But it's not meant to carry you beyond that initial push. This is where most people get stuck. They mistake willpower for a permanent fuel source, then feel like a failure when it fizzles out.

It's not your fault—it's just mental physics.

Let's say you get inspired after hearing a motivational speaker. You walk out of that seminar ready to conquer the world. You swear off sugar, commit to yoga, and decide you're going to write a book and become a minimalist by January 1st. You feel bulletproof... for a few days.

Then, a week later, you're eating Pop-Tarts in bed, watching re-runs, and wondering where that unstoppable energy went.

That energy really didn't go anywhere. It's there, but just wasn't designed to last. Willpower is great at saying "no" once or twice, but it gets tired quickly. It's like that friend who enthusiastically volunteers to help you move, but disappears the moment they hear the couch has to go up the steps.

When willpower runs out—as it inevitably does—you're left with your conscious mind, scrambling for a new strategy. And without support from the deeper subconscious mind, you'll likely revert to old habits and familiar patterns, because that's where the real programming lives.

So, yes, the conscious mind houses willpower, but real, lasting change happens when you reprogram the systems deeper within.

In other words, don't blame your willpower for being weak—it's just doing the job it was hired for, and that's merely giving you a boost. But for real transformation, you've got to hand over the controls to something much more powerful, the subconscious.

It Holds Our Short Term Memory

The final aspect of the conscious mind is its role as the keeper of our short-term memory. This is also known as "working memory." Think of it as the Post-it note section of your brain. It's where you temporarily store bits of information that are useful or needed right now, but not necessarily worth saving for the long haul.

Need to remember a phone number just long enough to dial it? That's your conscious mind at work. Making a grocery list in your head while you wander the supermarket aisles? Also your conscious mind. It's juggling information moment-to-moment, but only what's immediately relevant.

The conscious mind doesn't do long-term storage. It's more like a whiteboard that gets wiped clean regularly. If the information doesn't serve a current purpose, it's gone. That's why you can walk into a room and completely forget why you went in there. Your conscious mind dumped the "why" file because it figured it wasn't needed anymore, and now you're standing there like you've just been teleported into that room with no mission.

This short-term memory function is essential for decision-making in the present moment, but it's fleeting. It doesn't record your life, it just helps you manage the day-to-day, like that sticky note on the fridge. And if you want something to stick around longer, you've got to either repeat it often enough or get it past the Critical Faculty (coming up soon), and into the VIP lounge of your subconscious.

So yes, your conscious mind is doing some important juggling—but it's not writing anything in stone. More like scribbling in sand while the tide comes in.

That's All There Is

Well, that's everything your conscious mind does. Are you surprised? You're not alone. For something we treat like the CEO of our life, the conscious mind is more like the receptionist—

Joe **Hammer**

answering phones, making quick decisions, and trying to look busy. It handles our day-to-day awareness, helps us plan and analyze, makes snap decisions, and holds onto fleeting bits of information like a squirrel with a bad memory.

But when it comes to lasting transformation, emotional responses, deep-seated beliefs, and those pesky habits you just can't seem to shake—your conscious mind is almost entirely out of its depth. Even though it desires to lead the show, it's not the one writing the script. That's why we can know what we should do and still do the exact opposite ... like eating a pizza while reading an article about healthy living.

The conscious mind is the one we hear the loudest, but it's not the one running the deeper programming. For that, we need to look beneath the surface—into the vast, silent power of the subconscious, where the real action happens. It's the realm of automatic behavior, deeply rooted beliefs, and emotional responses that often defy logic.

And it's also the stomping ground of your Unconscious Authority.

So now that we've shaken hands with the receptionist, let's look behind the curtain and meet the one truly in charge.

Until you make the unconscious conscious, it will direct your life and you will call it fate.

Carl Jung

The Unconscious **Authority**

The Subconscious Mind – The Master Archive

The subconscious is our mind's master recording device. Think of it as the 24/7 surveillance system of your life—but way more accurate. It doesn't sleep, doesn't take coffee breaks, and never misses anything. It's the mind's massive storage unit—the kind that goes on forever. It's 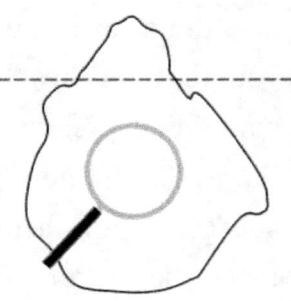 packed floor to ceiling with every suggestion, feeling, belief, emotion, image, and word you've encountered since your very first moment of existence. And for many, that even includes the moments before you were born.

Let's be clear:

- Every word you've heard.
- Every look someone gave you.
- Every childhood giggle, heartbreak, or birthday party snub.
- Every smell, every song, every awkward junior high dance.

Yes, all of it is encoded and archived with stunning precision in the subconscious mind.

And this isn't just dusty data sitting in storage. This information is active. It plays a major role in shaping your decisions, habits, emotions, and even your sense of identity, all without you consciously realizing it. Your subconscious is pulling the strings while your conscious mind is often left trying to make sense of the situation... "Wait... why did I do that again?"

But the subconscious is more than just a mental hard drive. It's also the intuitive, universal mind. The deeply connected part of you that reaches beyond your personal story and taps into something greater. Call it what you will—The Universe, God Force, Soul Energy, Higher Self, Divine Intelligence—it's the source of your deeper truths. It's where your truest desires originate, the seat of love, purpose, beauty, unity, and meaning.

This is the part of you that doesn't just store your memories—it knows your potential. It's not bogged down by logic or limited by what's "realistic." It's imaginative, boundless, and deeply powerful. And best of all...

It's Programmable!

Yes, the same mind that absorbed unfiltered childhood fears and beliefs is also capable of rewiring itself to serve your highest vision of who you are. When you understand how to work with this magnificent force—not just talk about change, but actually access the root system where real transformation happens—you move from "trying" to "becoming."

And that, my friend, is when the Unconscious Authority begins to wake up.

It's Timeless

Your subconscious is like a cosmic library living in your cells. Think of it as a dusty, ancient library stuffed with the wisdom

The Unconscious **Authority**

(and quirks) of your ancestors, encoded in your DNA. It's not flipping through books, though—it's quietly humming with cellular memory, a silent vibe of your entire backstory. Think of it as your brain's eccentric historian, hoarding every lesson from caveman days to now. No saber-toothed tigers are chasing you anymore, but tell that to your subconscious when you're stuck in traffic or facing a looming work deadline. It'll still scream, "DANGER!" and kick you into fight-or-flight mode.

Sometimes, it even overreacts to fake threats—like a nightmare about missing a flight or the sheer terror of public speaking. Your subconscious doesn't fact-check; it just drools adrenaline at you.

If your conscious mind is the architect, sketching out your grand plans, dreams, and to-do lists, your subconscious is the contractor who actually builds the thing—sometimes with a questionable sense of style. You tell it, "Let's be confident!" and it might nod, then sneakily build a wobbly shack of self-doubt because that's what it's used to. It's obsessed with actualizing whatever you focus on, whether it's a goal, a fear, or that one catchy jingle you can't unhear.

It's also a sensory sponge, soaking up sights, sounds, smells, feelings, and tastes. Feed it positive vibes, and it might construct a masterpiece. Dwell on gloom, and it's like hiring a contractor who only knows how to build haunted houses.

Your subconscious is a treasure trove of history, but it's not always the most reliable narrator. It can be your hype man, boosting you with instincts and intuition, or it can be that one friend who overreacts to everything. The trick is training it. Words help—like telling yourself, "I'm awesome!" ... however experiences are its true love language. You can lecture your subconscious about kindness all day, but if it grew up watching your parents bicker like an episode of Real Housewives, it's filing away that drama instead.

So, treat your subconscious like a slightly unhinged but lovable pet. Show it good examples, give it clear directions, and maybe don't let it binge-watch horror movies before bed. With a little TLC, it'll stop building panic shacks and start constructing the life you actually want!

It's Literal

Unlike the conscious mind's ability to fuss over every details, your subconscious is the stagehand who just executes the script, no questions asked. It doesn't pause to judge, weigh options, or ponder if the plot makes sense. It's a literal-minded workhorse, grabbing whatever instincts, habits, or dusty memories from your personal history it can find.

This stagehand doesn't care if the script is a feel-good movie or a horror flick. It has no built-in sense of right or wrong, no ethical filter, and definitely no knack for spotting red flags. Feed it a thought like, "I'm doomed to mess this up," and it's like, "Got it, cue the self-sabotage!"

Tell it, "I'm unstoppable," and it'll start building a superhero montage in your brain. It's not smart enough to reject bad ideas or pat itself on the back for good ones—it just takes whatever you give it and slaps it into the production. And unlike your conscious mind, which might dream up poetic goals or clever quips, the subconscious isn't out here writing original content. It's got no spark of inspiration or wisdom to offer; it's just a do-er, not a thinker.

The subconscious loves and is stimulated by imagination, however *it cannot be coerced or pressured to change by will.*

Trying to strong-arm your subconscious into behaving with sheer willpower is like trying to convince a cat to fetch your slippers. It doesn't respond to stern commands, motivational posters, or the mantras on your bathroom mirror. It's more like a stubborn artist who only works when inspired, and its muse is imagination.

Paint a vivid mental picture like you confidently nailing a speech or basking in a tropical vacation—and your subconscious lights up like a kid at a candy store, ready to turn that vision into reality. It thrives on sensory details... the sound of applause, the smell of ocean air, the rush of adrenaline.

But try to force it to change through discipline alone? It'll just cross its arms and say, "Nah, I'm sticking with my old script, thanks."

It loves the drama of vivid scenes and emotional vibes. For example, if you keep imagining yourself tripping over your words during a presentation, your subconscious will happily rehearse that flop, making you sweaty and stammer when the moment

Joe **Hammer**

arrives. But if you visualize yourself charming the socks off the audience, it'll start rigging the stage for success. The catch? You can't just tell it to change; you have to show it the new script through sensory-rich mental rehearsals.

Let's give a standing ovation to your subconscious for handling the grunt work of being human, because without it, you'd be a hot mess. Imagine if you had to consciously remind yourself to blink every few seconds, or micromanage your blood flow.... "Heart, pump now! Lungs, inhale—wait, not that fast!"

Your subconscious is the ultimate backstage crew, quietly running the show so you don't have to. It keeps your body temperature steady, so you're not sweating like your first hot yoga class or shivering like a chihuahua in a snowstorm. It handles swallowing to keep your throat from turning dry, and it even nudges you to scratch that random itch on your nose without you needing to utter a formal request.

Ever notice how you automatically shift in your chair when your butt starts being uncomfortable? Or how you yawn when you're tired without thinking about it? That's your subconscious carrying out millions of little tasks on its to-do list. From adjusting your posture, regulating your breathing, or making sure you don't choke on your coffee, it nails them all. This autopilot mode frees up your conscious mind to obsess over more important things, like watching that new Netflix series.

Your subconscious is a literal, no-nonsense worker who takes every thought, image, and habit as a direct order, however it will never win an award for critical thinking.

The Unconscious **Authority**

It's Not a Very Good Wordsmith

Let's start with one of the subconscious mind's little quirks—it doesn't understand negatives. It skips right over words like "not," "don't," and "never." So when you say, "I will not eat chocolate," your subconscious only hears "I will eat chocolate." Guess what happens next? You're elbow-deep in a bag of M&M's before you even realize it.

This is exactly why affirmations and subconscious suggestions must always be stated positively. You must tell the mind what to do, not what to avoid. Say, "I choose healthy foods that nourish my body," and your subconscious says, "Got it, boss!"—instead of sabotaging your efforts with unhealthy cravings.

It's Forever Youthful

Your subconscious never grows up. While your conscious mind has aged, gone to school, paid taxes, and learned how to use your computer, your subconscious is still back in the sandbox playing with Legos... and it remembers every moment quite vividly.

It's permanently parked in the now, meaning it doesn't perceive time like your conscious mind does. Yet the decisions it makes are based on old data, sometimes way old. If your six-year-old self heard "You'll never be good at math," your subconscious may still believe that's gospel truth, even if your adult self has outgrown it.

This means outdated beliefs—formed before you even had the

ability to think critically—could still be running your life. We are simply replaying our outdated historical recording in our daily lives. All fear has roots that are silently connected it to our past experiences.

Ernest Holmes, author of The Science of Mind once said, *"The universal mind contains all knowledge; It is the potential ultimate of all things. To it, all things are possible."*

That's not just poetic woo-woo—it's literal. This universal mind doesn't filter what's "good" for you. If you carry habitual, negative thoughts or disempowering beliefs, it will get to work on manifesting those just as efficiently as it would your best, brightest, most inspired desires.

If you consistently think negative thoughts or unconsciously cling to limiting beliefs, your subconscious will do everything in its power to make them come true.

It's a neutral genie with no moral compass and no judgment, just execution.

It's a Massive Storage Center

Your subconscious mind is the ultimate filing cabinet. It's a massive, hyper-organized, emotionally attuned storage system that houses everything you've ever experienced. Every word you've heard, every smell you've smelled, every song lyric you didn't even realize you knew. It's all there, cataloged and color-coded, ready to be retrieved the moment something in the present rings the right bell.

The Unconscious **Authority**

Psychologists estimate that over 95% of what you think, say, and do originates from this archived data. It's the original hard drive—one that never forgets. The subconscious is often referred to as the "elephant mind" because it retains everything. Even things your conscious mind would really prefer it didn't!

It records emotions, sensory experiences, beliefs, and decisions—good, bad, and questionable—and brings them forward into your present-day reality. It's like living in a movie where the past keeps sneaking into the script.

It's a Work-a-holic

Fatigue is an unknown experience to the subconscious mind as it never overworks or tires. It operates and oversees the mechanisms and physiological functions of our body, from regulating our heart rate to breathing, from organ functions to digestion. Studies suggest that more than 75% of our daily activities are regulated by the subconscious mind.

Think about this . . . your heart beats more than 100,000 times a day, pumping your blood through 60,000 miles of arteries, veins and capillaries—and it's all controlled without any conscious thought or involvement by you. Pretty amazing, right?

And yet we still have problems finding a street sign when the radio is too loud!

Joe Hammer

It is Reflective

Your subconscious doesn't just record and store... it mirrors. Whatever you radiate inwardly, whether that's judgment, fear, resentment, or love, gets reflected right back to you. It's not punishment; it's programming. You're seeing yourself in everything around you.

If you're harboring judgment or criticism toward others, that's not just damaging to your relationships, it's creating an inner environment of negativity that becomes your own lived experience. Think of it like a spiritual boomerang... whatever you throw out comes right back.

This is why people often find themselves repeating the same kinds of relationships, jobs, or emotional patterns. The subconscious mind is simply looping the old tape until it's told—clearly and positively—to record a new one. Even though it wields tremendous power, the subconscious mind is a servant of the conscious mind. It will follow orders, however those orders must match the existing programming in the subconscious or it will be rejected. (More on this when we discuss The Critical Factor).

The subconscious often represses memories having unresolved negative emotions attached to them. These memories may not be consciously recalled, but the beliefs and feelings associated with them will still influence your reactions to situations and circumstances in your life. Guilt, resentment, anger, fear and depression must be resolved at the subconscious level in order to deliver a reaction that is dissimilar to our conscious awareness.

The Unconscious **Authority**

It's Lazy

The subconscious mind is extremely lazy when it comes to making changes to the historic programming present within it. It enjoys following the path of least resistance.

As you've learned, it is busy around the clock. Unlike the conscious mind, which has the ability to rest when necessary and sleep at night, the subconscious mind continues its work 24 hours a day, seven days a week, 365 days a year. It has no time off. Your blood doesn't stop circulating when you go to bed. It is responsible for your body functions even when the conscious mind has checked out.

It Buries the Bad Stuff (but still acts on it)

The subconscious often represses memories that are painful, traumatic, or carry unresolved emotional weight. These memories may not be readily available to your conscious mind, but the feelings and beliefs tied to them still influence how you behave, what you believe about yourself, and how you react to the world around you.

So if you're wondering why you keep blowing up during some conversations, or freezing when asked to speak in a meeting—chances are, your subconscious is running a program from years ago. And you don't need to consciously remember the event for it to be affecting you.

The emotions, guilt, shame, anger, fear, resentment—will continue influencing your behavior until they're identified and resolved at the subconscious level.

This is the powerhouse you're working with. It's not just a mental filing cabinet—it's your deepest operating system. And while it's immensely powerful, it's also incredibly literal, deeply emotional, and sometimes stuck in the past.

It's the Residence for Habits, Beliefs and Emotions

Your subconscious is where all the real stuff lives—the *habits*, *beliefs*, and *emotions* that quietly run the show called your life.

Let's start with habits. These aren't just your morning coffee rituals or that charming tendency to scroll Instagram instead of doing something productive. Habits can also be habits of thought—and those are the sneaky ones. You don't notice them the same way you notice biting your nails or automatically checking if you locked the front door, but they're most often the real culprits when it comes to blocking progress in your relationships, health, and career.

So yes, that unconscious loop of "I'm not good enough," or "People like me don't succeed," is a habit. A thought-habit. And the subconscious has been carefully marinating in it for years, like a crockpot slowing preparing your favorite vegetable soup.

Now let's talk about *beliefs*. These are the silent architects of your reality. You didn't consciously choose them—most of them were installed early... by others. Beliefs determine what you accept as normal, acceptable, possible.

The Unconscious **Authority**

Remember when I mentioned sitting down to a dinner of "dog"? You didn't have to weigh pros and cons—you instantly rejected the idea. Why? Not because you paused to do a nutritional analysis, but because that thought didn't align with your belief system. The subconscious instantly said, "Nope! Not for me!"

This is why you can set bold conscious goals like "I'm going to start a business" or "I'm finally going to love myself," and then two days later you're binge-watching crime documentaries with a bag of chips wondering what happened. What happened is your belief structure said, "That's not who we are," and pulled you right back into the familiar.

Now, on to *emotions*—which, by the way, come from the Latin word *emovere*, meaning "to move through or out." That's literally what emotions do. They move energy through your body, often whether you like it or not.

Emotions are the body's reaction to the mind. They are physicalized expressions of what you believe to be true at a deep level. They can be the good guys (love, joy, inspiration, gratitude) or the ones you don't invite to parties (jealousy, rage, shame, grief, fear). But even the "bad" emotions have their uses.

Jealousy might nudge you to step up your game.

Anxiety might signal a problem that needs solving.

Sadness might slow you down just long enough to finally pay attention.

The challenge is that our conscious mind can't process emotions very well. It doesn't have the bandwidth. So, it does what any overwhelmed boss does—it delegates. It passes them down to the subconscious, which says, "Okay, I'll hang onto that for life."

Think about it. You're in a movie theater watching a fictional drama, and suddenly a tear rolls down your cheek. Why? You know it's not real. You know those are actors. But your subconscious? It doesn't care. It's not analyzing the script or checking the actors' backgrounds. It's experiencing the emotion as if it's happening right now. Because it lives in the now, and it takes everything literally.

That's why movies work. It's called the *"willing suspension of disbelief,"* a tiny hypnotic trance we all slip into. And it's why your subconscious doesn't know the difference between an emotional memory from 20 years ago and something happening today. It just reacts.

Ever felt uneasy walking into a room and had no clue why? It was likely related to the lighting, the color of the carpet, a faint smell... something your subconscious linked to an earlier, unpleasant experience. Consciously, you're like, "Huh, weird vibe in here." But subconsciously? Your system is already on alert, whispering, "Hey... we've seen this before. We don't like it. Be careful."

These emotional messages aren't always rational, but they are very real. And they affect everything... your mood, your decisions, your gut feelings. Your subconscious is constantly scanning your environment for clues and patterns, trying to protect

The Unconscious **Authority**

you... even if it's using outdated data.

Your subconscious is simply the cozy home of your habits, the firm seat of your beliefs, and the deep vault of your emotions. It does all this behind the scenes, without asking for permission—and without needing you to understand why.

And that's why transformation doesn't just happen by "thinking positively." You have to get into the subconscious, speak its language, and retrain the resident. Otherwise, your thoughts will just keep knocking politely at the door while your old programming chills on the couch eating Doritos, completely ignoring them.

It's the Protector (with a Slightly Overactive Imagination)

Last but definitely not least, the subconscious mind is your ever-vigilant protector. It's like having your own built-in bodyguard, only instead of wearing sunglasses and an earpiece, it's constantly scanning your environment for anything that even remotely resembles danger—physical, emotional, or otherwise.

However, it's not super sophisticated. Think of it like a highly loyal dog that can sniff out fear but doesn't quite understand context. It will act on whatever it believes is dangerous, even if that danger isn't a viable threat.

Importantly, and this is key... *it doesn't know the difference between something real and something vividly imagined.*

Let me explain...

Joe **Hammer**

Say you're out on a peaceful hike, birds chirping, nature doing its thing—and suddenly, a grizzly bear steps out onto the trail. Do you pause and consult your internal library of wildlife documentaries? Nope. You don't sit down for a TED Talk with yourself about bear protocol. What happens is instantaneous. Your heart rate skyrockets, adrenaline floods your system, and you become The Flash in hiking boots. That's your subconscious protection system doing what it does best... keeping you alive, no questions asked.

However, that same exact reaction can happen if you just dream about a bear. If you've ever woken up from a nightmare sweating, heart racing, and glancing suspiciously around your bedroom for signs of wildlife, then congratulations, you've met your subconscious in full emergency mode.

Your subconscious doesn't fact-check. It doesn't look for disclaimers like, "Relax, this is just a dream," or "Hey, this is only a memory from 1994." *It reacts based on belief, not reality.*

This protective instinct is powerful but often misguided. Your subconscious acts as a nervous system "safety valve." When something happens that causes you emotional distress, especially during childhood. It locks that memory away for safekeeping. Then it stands ready to alert you if anything similar ever happens again. Even if it's decades later.

Your subconscious has no sense of time. As far as it's concerned, you're still five years old, still vulnerable, still needing protection. So when something feels similar to a past wound,

The Unconscious **Authority**

the alarm goes off. Except it doesn't tell you why. It just flips the switch, triggering that "uh-oh" feeling... from mild unease to a full-on panic attack.

It's like your subconscious is yelling, "Warning! This might hurt you like that other thing did!" And your conscious mind is left going, "Wait, what other thing?"

And that is the frustrating part. The subconscious trips the safety valve, but the original cause of the alarm is buried deep... a long-lost receipt from your emotional past. All you know is that you're suddenly on edge, uncomfortable, or spiraling—and you don't know why.

To make matters worse, the subconscious is extremely creative in how it attempts to protect you. It will make you avoid certain people, self-sabotage opportunities, or get irrationally angry at totally minor things. It's trying to keep you safe—just doing so in the most roundabout and sometimes very awkward ways possible.

Like a pressure cooker with that little valve on top that hisses when it's had enough pressure, your subconscious has a built-in system to release tension. That's how your subconscious works. When the emotional pressure builds up, it pops the lid a bit—only instead of steam, you get a tight chest, a racing mind, or an inexplicable desire to punch something.

So if you've ever said, "I don't know why I'm feeling this way," you're not broken. You're just dealing with a very old, very loyal part of your mind trying to keep you safe... based on outdated data.

Joe **Hammer**

Yesterday's Events, Today's Overreactions

Let's talk about why you sometimes feel like you're losing your mind over something that, on the surface, seems totally harmless—like getting nervous before a work presentation or irrationally upset when someone utters a comment.

First off, understand something... It's not about that moment at all. *It's about what your subconscious remembers.*

Deep in the vault of your subconscious, there's something called the ISE, or *Initial Sensitizing Event*. This is the moment—usually tucked somewhere in your childhood—when something happened that made you feel hurt, scared, abandoned, judged, powerless, etc. It might've seemed minor at the time... or maybe it was a big deal... but either way, your subconscious recorded it as "Danger! We must never feel this again!"

The challenging part is that you probably don't even remember the original event. But your subconscious? Oh, it remembers.

Now, fast-forward to adulthood. You experience something—a situation, a tone of voice, a smell, a facial expression—that feels vaguely like that old, buried ISE. Your subconscious reacts, "Uh-oh... this reminds me of that time," and slaps down another layer of emotional memory on top of the original.

These follow-up memories are called SSEs—*Subsequent Sensitizing Events*. They're like emotional déjà vu. Every time something feels even remotely similar to the ISE, your subconscious adds another notch to the tally.

The Unconscious **Authority**

Let's make it visual...

Imagine your ISE is the very first pancake in a tall, syrupy stack. Fresh, hot, and full of trauma! Every time you experience another SSE—another emotionally charged moment that your subconscious thinks is even slightly related—it adds another pancake to the pile.

Over time, you're walking around with a sky-high emotional pancake stack inside you. It's tall, unstable, and soaked in subconscious syrup. You don't see it, but your nervous system is carrying the weight.

Eventually, someone makes an offhand comment... or you're put in a mildly stressful situation... or a smell reminds you of something you can't quite place, and BAM!, the whole stack topples over.

Suddenly you're having a panic attack in a grocery store aisle or snapping at someone you love, and you don't even know why. Consciously, nothing makes sense. But subconsciously? That moment just added the last unstable pancake to an already wobbly tower.

When your subconscious sends out the "danger!" alert, it's not trying to ruin your day. It genuinely thinks it's helping. It's trying to protect you from reliving that ISE—the original wound.

But because it can't reason or analyze, it just reacts. Think of it like an overprotective parent who won't let you go near the kiddie pool because you could drown. The intention is good. The logic? Not so much.

Joe **Hammer**

So these subconscious reactions, while very real in the moment, are often based on outdated, misinterpreted, or flat-out irrelevant data. You're dealing with a full-blown defense system that was programmed by a 5-year-old version of you who was just trying to survive.

And unless the ISE and SSEs are uncovered, processed, and updated—like the latest version of your computer's operating system—you'll keep getting those unhelpful alerts and malfunctions.

Phobias

Phobias are born out of intense emotional moments—moments that often don't even register in our conscious memory. But rest assured, your subconscious remembers everything. Like a hypervigilant bodyguard with a photographic memory and zero sense of logic, it locked those moments away as if to say, "We're never doing that again."

Let's look at an example..

Mary and John were planning a dream anniversary trip to Hawaii. Cue the palm trees, sunsets, umbrella drinks—and then cue disaster. A week before the trip, Mary came down with a brutal illness that left her bedridden. She felt terrible—not just physically, but emotionally. She knew John was looking forward to the break from his stressful job, and now, because of her, the whole trip was canceled. Guilt piled on top of the fever.

Fast-forward a few weeks. They're rebooking the trip, and suddenly Mary finds herself panicking. Her heart races. Her palms

The Unconscious **Authority**

sweat. She can't breathe. She's developed a full-blown fear of flying. And that fear of flying remained with her decades later.

Why? Because her subconscious connected that horrible sickness not to the illness, but to the plane ride.

Does that make any logical sense? Of course not. But the subconscious mind doesn't do logic. It doesn't weigh pros and cons or review flight safety records. It just reacts. In this case, it slapped a big "danger" sticker on flying, all in the name of protecting her from repeating what *it* thinks made her sick. Good intention, bad data.

And that's how phobias are formed... emotionally charged events from the past—especially in childhood—get locked in as truth, and then those events echo back as irrational fears in adulthood.

If your older brother once locked you in a closet when you were four, your tiny mind might've screamed, "I'm going to die in here!" That panic, locked in by your subconscious, can grow up into claustrophobia—an adult fear of tight spaces.

If you took a tumble out of a treehouse as a kid, heights might now make your knees weak, even if you're just standing on a sturdy balcony.

Or take little Joanne. At four years old, she visited her sick grandma in the hospital. When she asked if Grandma would be okay, a well-meaning doctor tried to soothe her, "Don't worry, it's just pneumonia." But Grandma didn't make it. Joanne grew up with *Iatrophobia*—fear of doctors, also known as "white coat syndrome." Her subconscious wasn't scared of pneumonia, it was scared of being lied to... and losing someone she loved.

Again, none of these fears are logical. They're emotional reflexes, rooted in your brain's old, overprotective operating system. These are classic fight-or-flight responses that don't match the present-day reality—but your subconscious doesn't care. It doesn't know that you're not four years old anymore, or that a medical checkup isn't a death sentence.

Until we uncover the Initial Sensitizing Event (ISE) and any Subsequent Sensitizing Events (SSEs)—those emotionally charged roots of the problem—the faulty alarm system keeps firing.

Your subconscious is insanely powerful. But it doesn't run on logic. It runs on literal interpretation. It's like a Secret Service agent on permanent red alert, interpreting every shadow as a potential threat. You won't even know it's working—it prefers to operate in stealth mode. But it's always on duty.

That's why something that seems insignificant on the surface can turn into a major life obstacle. The subconscious doesn't care how big or small the original event was. It only cares that something felt threatening, and it's going to make damn sure you avoid that feeling again.

Take one of my clients, for example. He came to me with a rough case of IBS. He'd seen doctors, nutritionists—you name it. He was on every diet known to man, no coffee, no chocolate, no nuts, no fried foods, no joy.

The Unconscious **Authority**

None of it worked.

Finally, he tried a regressive hypnosis session with me. And what did we find beneath all the food charts and GI jargon? One simple, powerful culprit...*worry*.

Turns out, he had grown up in a wildly unstable home environment, and his subconscious had learned early on that worrying 24/7 was his best shot at staying emotionally safe. That habitual worry had been burning in the background for years, eventually expressing itself through his gut. His symptoms weren't caused by bananas or brownies—they were caused by an overactive thought pattern.

Once we uncovered the ISE and SSEs driving his subconscious to hold onto worry like a security blanket, he was able to release it. The result? His IBS cleared almost immediately.

A few weeks later, he told me that he'd gained three pounds from finally enjoying all the foods he'd been forbidden to eat. He tagged it, "The best three pounds of my life!"

The Critical Faculty

Let's meet the last key player in the drama of your mind: *The Critical Faculty*, also known as the *Critical Factor*, the inner skeptic, or that little voice in your head that constantly asks, "Wait... does this make sense?"

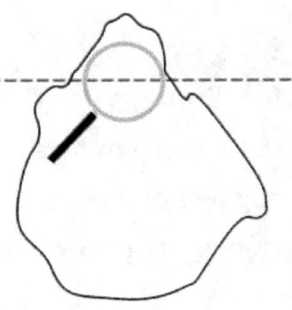

Joe **Hammer**

Think of it as the gatekeeper to your subconscious mind. Its job? To judge every single piece of incoming information—whether it's something you see, hear, read, or feel—and decide if it should be allowed in or shown the door.

This process happens lightning-fast. As soon as your senses deliver new information, the Critical Faculty jumps into action, holding it up against the massive database of your personal life experience and asks, "Does this match what we already believe to be true?"

If the answer is yes—ding ding ding!—the info is welcomed into the subconscious like a long-lost friend. If the answer is no, it gets blocked faster than a unwanted sales call during dinner.

Imagine your subconscious mind as a giant warehouse, filled with the boxes of your memories, beliefs, and everything you've ever experienced. The Critical Faculty is the bouncer at the door with a clipboard, checking every new thought or suggestion against the VIP list of your established beliefs.

If something matches? It's waved right in. If not? "Sorry. You're rejected."

Let's say I again suggested you consider trying that dog meat for dinner. Your Critical Faculty slams the brakes on that faster than you could say "pass the soy sauce." Why? Because that suggestion conflicts with your beliefs, culture, or personal experience. It simply doesn't resonate—and boom, it gets rejected.

The Unconscious **Authority**

It's a Lazy Gatekeeper

Your Critical Faculty doesn't fully exist when you're a kid. It starts forming somewhere between the ages of 9 and 11. Before that? The subconscious is like a wide-open field, and everything—good, bad, magical, or downright bizarre—marches straight in without resistance.

This is why kids can believe in Santa Claus and the Tooth Fairy. It's also why they can absorb more harmful beliefs, like "I'm stupid," "I'm unlovable," or "I'll never be good enough." These early suggestions go straight into the subconscious with zero questioning, often setting up emotional roadblocks that last a lifetime.

Sure, the Santa thing fades thanks to older kids on the playground, but those internalized "truths" about the self? They tend to stick around and become part of the mental furniture.

Even though the Critical Faculty is always on duty, it's not exactly a go-getter. It's a bit of a lazy guard. More of a "don't rock the boat" type. It prefers to maintain the status quo—even if that status quo is limiting you.

This is why changing deep beliefs can be so hard. Even when new information would clearly be beneficial—like "Hey, maybe I'm actually good enough"—the Critical Faculty might shut it down simply because it doesn't match the outdated info in storage.

In other words, it's loyal to your past—not your potential.

Joe **Hammer**

It's Lightning Fast in Making Decisions

Let me show you just how fast your Critical Faculty does its job. Seriously, it's like the Formula One pit crew of your mind—blisteringly fast, constantly alert, and a little bit smug about how much it knows.

Ready? Okay...

This is the number seven: **8**

Boom! Did you feel that? That little mental jolt? That was your Critical Faculty jumping out of its chair like, "Hold up! That's not seven! That's eight!"

You didn't have to Google it. You didn't need to phone a friend. You just knew—instantly and instinctively—that what I said was wrong. That's because your Critical Faculty compared what I told you ("this is the number seven") to the wealth of information already stored in your subconscious... those years of math classes, Sesame Street episodes, and grocery aisle price tags. And the result?

Rejected... like a bad Tinder match.

Now, contrast that with a toddler. If I told a two-year-old that "8" is the number seven, there's a good chance they'd nod and accept it without question—because their Critical Faculty hasn't been fully installed yet. Their little minds are wide open for download. They're still building their mental database, so their inner gatekeeper hasn't quite learned to say, "Wait a second..."

The Unconscious **Authority**

But you? You've got years of "eightness" under your belt. That shape, those curves—your mind has seen it too many times to be fooled now.

So yes, your Critical Faculty is fast. In fact, it's too fast sometimes. It doesn't stop to check whether an old belief is still serving you—it just asks, "Does this match what we already know?" If yes, it lets it in. If not, it slams the door faster than you can say "self-sabotage."

The Communication System

Let's talk about how your conscious and subconscious minds communicate... They don't.

They do not speak the same language. One's like a high-powered radio announcer, and the other's more like a silent ninja running the control room of your body 24/7—without needing your permission or input. However, both minds are excellent at what they do, but they operate in completely different ways.

Take your subconscious—it handles all your behind-the-scenes operations. Breathing, blinking, digesting, circulating blood, keeping your heart beating—it's the ultimate multitasker. And it does all this without sending you a single memo. Imagine if you could hear it:

"Hey! Don't forget to blink!"

Joe **Hammer**

"Time to swallow that saliva—you're not a camel!"

"Quick heart check—yep, still pumping!"

"Kidneys, status report?"

Yeah... you'd go bananas in a couple days of uttering this nonsense.

Luckily, your subconscious works in silence, like the world's most loyal personal assistant. It runs the show backstage so your conscious mind can focus on life's big decisions—like which cereal to buy or whether you can pull off that new pair of skinny jeans.

Your conscious mind, on the other hand, is chatty. You can actually hear it thinking. It narrates your day like it's auditioning for a podcast. For example:

"This shirt would go great with those jeans I bought last week."

"Ooh, it's on sale. I'm basically making money."

"Wait... this syrup is like 90% high-fructose corn sugar sludge. Hard pass."

Sound familiar?

Some folks even take it up a notch and narrate these thoughts out loud in public. If you've ever stood in line at Walmart behind someone talking to themselves like they're co-hosting a morning talk show, then you know what I'm talking about.

While your conscious mind is busy thinking, analyzing, planning, and talking to itself, it can't actually hear (or interrupt) the commands coming from your subconscious. That system runs silently—and automatically. Which means you're not reasoning with it or fact-checking what it's doing in real-time.

That's why your subconscious can sneak in beliefs and behaviors that make zero logical sense... and your conscious mind just goes along for the ride.

The Unconscious Authority's Training Methods

Let's take a look at a few of the most common ways our subconscious mind is trained, thus putting it in the position to silently control our lives ...

Repetition.

So how does the subconscious learn? How does it get programmed in the first place?

Repetition.

If you want to know how the UA got so good at running your life behind the scenes, just think back to elementary school—those endless multiplication tables. You didn't reason your way into knowing that 6 x 7 = 42. You repeated it. Over and over. Until it was burned into your brain like a bad TV commercial jingle.

That's exactly how subconscious training works.

Whether intentional or not, repetition creates neural pathways—basically highways of thought your brain uses out of habit. Think of it like carving grooves into your mental record. Play it enough times, and that groove becomes your default soundtrack.

Here's a real-life example:

You wake up, stretch, and think, "Ugh. It's going to be a long, miserable day." Later, your boss emails you about additional duties needing done. You sigh. Your coffee's lukewarm. The printer jams.

"Yep," you say, "just like I thought... a crummy day."

Repeat that cycle enough mornings, and guess what? Your subconscious accepts this gloomy little mantra as truth. It starts running "Bad Day at the Office" on repeat, even before your feet hit the floor.

Soon, you're not just having bad days—you're expecting them. Complaining about them. Dreading them. And your subconscious, loyal as ever, says, "Got it, boss. Another bad one coming right up."

So whether it's times tables, traffic rants, or telling yourself your job stinks, the subconscious doesn't care if the repetition is helpful or harmful. It just takes notes and builds habits accordingly.

Emotional Events

Your emotions aren't just fleeting reactions—they're the Uncon-

The Unconscious **Authority**

scious Authority's favorite way of taking notes. Big emotions act like highlighters for the subconscious. Any time you feel a strong emotional charge—fear, shame, love, excitement, humiliation, heartbreak—the subconscious perks up, grabs its Sharpie, and starts underlining whatever's happening in that moment.

Why? Because the subconscious assumes that if it was a high-emotion moment, it must be important for your survival. It doesn't stop to ask, "Is this healthy or helpful?" Nope—it just says, "Noted! Let's lock this in for life."

Emotional programming can happen from things that seem trivial—or from things we don't even remember. But if you felt something strongly in the moment, and someone said something that stuck, it likely carved out a little groove in your subconscious. And that groove is probably still playing the same old track today.

We see the present through the lens of our past.
Joe Hammer

Identification Statements

Let's shift gears and talk about the kind of programming that sneaks in not with drama, but with repetition—and often, with a smile.

As kids, we absorbed everything. And our parents? They were like the loudest radio station in town—broadcasting 24/7. What they said shaped how we saw ourselves and the world, even if they didn't mean for it to. Statements like:

"You're just like your mother—you want everything you see."

"You've got your father's temper."

"You'll never be good at math."

"You're the messy one in the family."

Even if these comments were made in jest—or out of frustration—they often stuck. And the subconscious didn't catch the sarcasm. It didn't say, "Ha! That was a good one, Dad!" It just quietly filed the message under Personal Truth, stamped it with "Approved by Someone I Trust," and moved on.

Now, I'm not saying your parents were villains. Most of them were doing their best with what they had. I'm not even calling it "bad parenting." (Although... occasionally, it might've been.)

But the truth is, even well-meaning parents can unintentionally hand out mental luggage that their kids carry for decades.

In my sessions, I'll sometimes ask clients about their childhood. The reaction is almost always defensive, "I had great parents!"

Great! But give it time. A little deeper into the conversation, we start uncovering things like this...

One woman couldn't understand why she obsessed over lists and order in her adult life. Turns out, her dad had a military-grade obsession with her childhood chore chart. Every task had

The Unconscious **Authority**

to be done his way, right away. No wiggle room.

Again—not a bad parent. Just a parent asserting responsibility. But the subconscious didn't interpret that as "Dad wants me to learn structure." It recorded: "If I'm not in control, I'm unsafe." Boom. Adult control issues, courtesy of Tuesday night dish duty.

Here's a lighter (and tastier) example:

I was out to dinner at a buffet with some friends. One guy in our group—let's call him "Buffet Bill"—was first in line. He loaded up his plate like he was competing in the Hunger Games, then sprinted to the table and started eating like it was his last meal on earth. By the time the rest of us made it through the line, he was licking his plate clean.

Later, over drinks, I teased him about his Olympic-speed dinner routine. His response?

"I grew up with six siblings. If you didn't eat fast, you didn't eat at all."

Ahhh. There it was. The Unconscious Authority in action.

Even though we were at an all-you-can-eat buffet with zero risk of starvation, his subconscious was still running the childhood script... Eat now or go hungry.

He laughed about it and admitted he'd never made that connection. But once he saw it, he got it. His adult behavior wasn't about manners or logic—it was about outdated programming running in the background, completely undetected.

Joe **Hammer**

So now that we've cracked open the vault and you see that childhood isn't off-limits, and that none of this is about parent-blaming or trauma-digging for sport, let's keep going. Your past doesn't define you—but understanding it gives you a whole lot more say in your future.

Now, the final frontier of training the Unconscious Authority...

Hypnosis - (And no, it's not clucking like a chicken)

Now we've come to the final and most fascinating method the Unconscious Authority uses to absorb programming—hypnosis. And before your mind jumps to swinging pocket watches or someone on stage spewing out deep, dark secrets, take a breath. That's Hollywood's version. What I'm talking about is something much more useful—and way less quacky.

I've spent years researching hypnosis, working with clients, and using regressive hypnotherapy to help people untangle the deep-rooted mental stuff that's been tripping them up for decades. The results? Let's just say hypnosis has a front-row seat in my toolkit for transformation.

In fact, hypnosis has been around for thousands of years, helping people heal, grow, and uncover what's buried beneath the surface. And it's not just "woo-woo" anymore. In 1958, the American Medical Association gave hypnosis a thumbs-up as a legitimate adjunct to medical care. So if doctors are cool with it, maybe it's time for you to raise an eyebrow of interest.

The Unconscious **Authority**

Talk Therapy Sometimes Falls Short

Traditional talk therapy? It's great. Necessary, even. But often, it's like trying to water the roots of a tree by misting the leaves. You talk, you analyze, you relive emotional wounds at the conscious level—and that's helpful to an extent. But the deepest material, the real stuff that's influencing your thoughts and behaviors? That's all happening way below the surface, where the Unconscious Authority is calling the shots.

Your conscious mind is like the face you show at the dinner party—smiling, sociable, and trying to appear in control. But your subconscious is the guy in the kitchen, quietly setting fire to the roast and wondering why the smoke alarm won't shut off. If you don't go into the kitchen, you can't fix the problem.

That's where hypnosis shines. Forget what you saw in that one movie where someone turns into a zombie after hearing a trigger word. Real hypnosis is simply a natural, focused state of awareness. You're not asleep. You're not under anyone's control. You're just very, very focused—so much so that you temporarily tune out the mental noise and access the part of your mind where lasting change happens.

And no, I don't have a swinging watch.

When you're in this focused state, you can make deep, meaningful changes to how you think, feel, and act. Hypnosis has been successfully used to treat everything from pain and depression to anxiety, stress, habits, jealousy, fear of flying, weird food cravings, and basically any area where your subconscious has decided to take the wheel and drive you off course.

Why it Works... Straight to the Source

Your subconscious is incredibly powerful—but it's also literal. It doesn't reason or negotiate. If it's told something with emotional weight, especially during a sensitizing event, it stamps that moment as "truth" and files it in a vault. That vault may be sealed off from your conscious awareness, but its contents still affect your daily life.

And guess what? Talk therapy can't always access that vault. Hypnosis can.

Through regressive hypnotherapy, we're able to tap into those original experiences via the Initial Sensitizing Event (ISE) and the Subsequent Sensitizing Events (SSEs) that formed your subconscious beliefs.

These are the pivotal moments that shaped how you see yourself, others, and the world. Sometimes, clients are shocked by what we uncover...

"Wait... That's it? That little moment from when I was six is why I keep sabotaging relationships?!"

Yes. Sometimes the most seemingly insignificant childhood experiences come with just enough emotion and suggestion to etch a lifetime of patterns into your subconscious.

The Unconscious **Authority**

But the good news is—once we uncover and deactivate the emotional charge around that event, your Unconscious Authority loosens its grip. That reaction you've been having over and over? Gone. The urge to control, the fear, the overeating, the jealousy—it no longer makes sense to your subconscious once the original "why" has been released.

Once the old programming is exposed and released, we can install new, useful subconscious instructions—ones that serve your best and highest good. You don't need to carry outdated mental baggage just because it was packed for you in childhood.

And if that lens is smudged with fear, shame, or outdated beliefs, then everything you see in the present—and everything you expect from the future—gets distorted.

Hypnosis helps you clean the lens. Or better yet, swap it out entirely.

So, now that you understand the immense potential of hypnosis—not as entertainment, but as a powerful tool for change—we're ready to dive into the Seven Mind Maxims, the operating principles of your quirky, brilliant, and occasionally stubborn mind.

Once you grasp these maxims, you'll begin to understand exactly how—and why—your Unconscious Authority works the way it does. Ready to peek behind the curtain? Let's go!

Joe **Hammer**

Maxims of the Mind

During my training in regressive hypnosis, I picked up some curious facts about the mind—curious, yes, but also incredibly useful. I've boiled them down into what I call *Mind Maxims*. A maxim is simply a "principle or rule of conduct," and in the realm of the Unconscious Authority, these aren't just guidelines—they're the law of the land; unshakable truths from the mind's mysterious playbook. Think of them as the mental "Terms & Conditions" you didn't know you agreed to, but you're definitely living by. Let's dive in...

Mind Maxim #1—What You Think About You'll Bring About

Whether real, imagined, dreamt or fabricated, our minds respond to mental images. These images then become our game plan for fulfillment.

A black cloud of negative thought will deliver dark, negative results every time. Conversely, when you internalize positive mental thoughts and expectancies, you tend to experience enjoyable, positive and energized results associated with that mindset. Your health is greatly dependent upon your mental expectancy. The expectations you carry about life live in the subconscious—quietly pulling strings and shaping outcomes.

Your physical well-being is also dependent upon your mental expectancy. There is always a mental expectancy in place, but it isn't always recognized by the conscious mind. Instead, it holds residence in our subconscious.

The Unconscious **Authority**

Just like a placebo (an innocent sugar pill) can actually make people feel better, your mental expectations have power. There's also something called *the nocebo effect,* where a person believes something will go wrong, and voila, it does. The mind is a magician, and belief is its favorite trick.

Mind Maxim #2—We Hold Our Beliefs to Be True

Thoughts become habits—and those habits of thought become the internal programs that guide our lives. Most of what we do isn't because we "thought it through," but because we've been conditioned to respond that way. It's habit, not high-level reasoning.

Once a belief finds a home in your subconscious, it sticks around like an old recliner you can't seem to throw away.

Take smoking. People say, "I smoke to relax." But nicotine is a stimulant, not a relaxant. So how does that make sense? It doesn't—but the belief is there, and the subconscious takes it as gospel. Logic doesn't matter.

Even beliefs that have been around forever can be updated. The longer they've been hanging around, the more effort it may take—but your subconscious can be reprogrammed. You just need the right tools.

Mind Maxim #3—Emotionally-Based Symptoms Can Cause Physical Outcomes

There are tons of scientific studies that confirm that if you experienced something emotionally harmful in the past, it can show up in your body today as illness, imbalance, or even disease.

Studies estimate that up to 70% of your ailments are caused by the nervous system's reaction to faulty subconscious programming, not something organic. Your subconscious doesn't know the difference between emotional stress and actual danger. It reacts the same way.

And this means that sometimes, what's hurting you physically might not be a virus or other illness, it might be an old memory that's overstayed its welcome.

Mind Maxim #4—Every Thought Motivates a Physical Reaction

Think about slicing a juicy lemon and popping it into your mouth. Really picture it. Feel that zing? That saliva is real. So is your body's response to fear or stress.

Holding on to resentment, fear, or guilt? Your body's not just sitting there quietly; it's reacting. Your thoughts are sending signals, and your nervous system is following orders.

That tight chest, that stomach knot, that grinding jaw? That's your body translating emotions into physical form. And when you realize that thoughts with emotional charge get stored in the subconscious, it becomes clear that if you want to change the physical effects, you've got to go back and deal with the original emotional event.

We become what we think about.

The Unconscious **Authority**

Thoughts with emotional energy attached to them reside deeply in the subconscious mind and will produce reactions consistent to those thoughts. To eradicate the reactions, one must reach the events responsible for initiating the feeling responsible for the reaction.

This isn't about wishful thinking. It's about getting down to the emotional wiring and flipping the right switch through access to the deeper, subconscious mind.

Mind Maxim #5—Imagination Trumps Knowledge

Images reside in the subconscious mind. Remember, the subconscious doesn't know the difference between what is real and what is vividly imagined. It has no reasoning. If you've ever experienced an expressive dream where your life was in danger, you'll remember how you suddenly awoke, sweating, your heart racing—even though you were safe in your bed.

So even if your conscious mind knows something isn't true, if the subconscious feels that it is... game over. But this is actually good news, because imagination is the gateway to change. Attach the right emotion to a new idea, and the subconscious is open to reprogramming. The old, dark beliefs can give way to something lighter and brighter!

Think of it this way: the subconscious doesn't respond to facts—it responds to feeling.

Mind Maxim #6—Subconscious Programming Cannot Be Forced

You cannot brute-force your subconscious into change. The harder you push, the more it digs in. Ever try to will yourself to sleep when you're wide awake? Yeah, it doesn't work.

Your critical faculty, that part of the mind that filters out what doesn't match past experiences, will swat away any suggestion that doesn't line up with your subconscious programming. That's why saying affirmations like "I am calm" while your heart's racing like a squirrel on espresso doesn't work. The subconscious isn't buying it.

To really change the program, you need to bypass the critical gatekeeper. That means reaching the subconscious in a calm, focused, and suggestible state through hypnosis. That's when the Unconscious Authority is most open to suggestion.

Mind Maxim #7—The Older the Habit, the More Difficult it is to Break

Whether it's a habit of thought, or a physical habit such as smoking or overeating, once it takes hold, a habit becomes more and more challenging to break as time goes by.

Going as far back as your early childhood experiences, historically formed habits are active in your life today. Try convincing yourself that $2 + 2 = 5$. Can't do it, right? That's because it's programmed in. It's not just what you know—it's what your subconscious believes.

The Unconscious **Authority**

But here's the hopeful part... *even the oldest habits can be changed.* They may have some serious roots, but with the right tools and approach you'll soon be discovering, you can uproot what no longer serves you... *and plant something far better in its place.*

> Your beliefs become your thoughts,
> Your thoughts become your words,
> Your words become your actions,
> Your actions become your habits,
> Your habits become your values,
> Your values become your destiny.
>
>
> Mahatma Gandhi

JOE'S NOTE ON: HABIT PATTERNS

Habits live in your subconscious, quietly steering the wheel while you think you're the one driving.

Many believe they are consciously choosing their behaviors each day, but in reality, a large portion of what we do is driven by automatic patterns deeply embedded in our subconscious minds.

Because the subconscious doesn't require our permission to act on a habit, it can lead us to repeat behaviors that no longer serve us.

Want to stop procrastinating? Eat healthier? Be more patient in your relationship? That's not just about "deciding" to change, it's about rewiring the internal script that's running the show.

This is why willpower often fails; we're trying to overpower a pattern that's operating below our level of awareness. It's like trying to change a ship's direction with a canoe paddle!

In both personal and business relationships, these subconscious habits can have major consequences. For instance, if your default reaction to criticism is defensiveness, it might sabotage honest communication with a partner or team member.

Recognizing that these habits are programmed responses provides you with the insight that you can't change what you're not aware of.

CHAPTER FIVE
The Client Files

By now, you've gotten to know the Unconscious Authority, that behind-the-scenes operator working overtime to protect us, often using outdated intel and emotional knee-jerk reactions stored deep in the subconscious.

You've also seen how this inner "security guard" sometimes acts less like a wise protector and more like someone who's trying to join a Zoom call with their fax machine.

Now, let's bring this to life.

I'm going to share a handful of real-life examples from my own client files; stories from people just like you and me who were living with challenges they didn't quite understand… until they took a look beneath the surface. Some of these long-standing beliefs had been hanging around like emotional wallpaper since childhood. Others seemed to sneak in overnight, causing chaos with no obvious explanation.

These are genuine breakthroughs and transformations I've witnessed firsthand in my work with regressive hypnosis. The names have been changed, of course, but the stories—and the shifts—are very real. As you read these examples, keep two things in mind:

Joe **Hammer**

- How the Unconscious Authority is attempting to protect the individual, and
- How those protective efforts are often based on faulty, outdated, or even laughably insignificant historic events that the subconscious took way too seriously.

Let's dive in—you might just recognize a piece of yourself in these stories!

The Postmaster and the Barbie Doll

Cindy came to me feeling trapped in a wave of anxiety, the kind that makes no logical sense. Everything in her life looked like it was going great. She had worked at the U.S. Postal Service for years, and one day her supervisor approached her with exciting news... she was the top candidate being considered for a Postmaster position at another branch.

She was thrilled. She rushed home to tell her husband. Then she shared it with friends, relatives — everyone. It was a well-earned promotion, and she was proud.

But as the date for her transfer approached, the excitement faded and was slowly replaced by something heavier... anxiety, nervousness, sleeplessness, tightness in the chest. This wasn't your standard case of "butterflies." It was deeper, harder to shake, and didn't match how she consciously felt.

"I know I can do the job," Cindy said to me in our intake interview. "I've been doing this work for years. I was chosen for a

The Unconscious **Authority**

reason." She smiled as she said it, but I could see the tears forming in her eyes. Her posture was tight. Her voice shook slightly when she spoke. Her words said confidence, but her body told a different story.

That's when I knew we weren't dealing with a conscious issue. This was the Unconscious Authority at work — her internal security system, sounding the alarm. The part of the mind that doesn't operate with logic or reason, but with emotionally coded memories. Her subconscious had detected a perceived "threat," and it was protecting her the only way it knew how... anxiety.

I guided her into a relaxed state, then gave the suggestion to her subconscious:

"Bring up the emotion you're feeling now — this anxiety — and take us back to the very first time in your life when you ever felt this way."

Within seconds, she began softly crying.

"I'm four years old," she said through tears.

"What's happening?" I asked gently.

"I'm sitting on the floor, playing with my Barbie doll."

Tears continued to stream down her face.

"Are you alone?"

"Yes," she whispered. "I invited two of my friends over to play, but... they laughed at me. Now they're in the other room playing without me."

"Why are they laughing?"

"Because I only have one Barbie and two outfits. They have lots of Barbies... and a suitcase full of clothes."

Her sobbing intensified.

"They made fun of me. Said I was poor. Said my doll was ugly."

There it was. The origin... the Initial Sensitizing Event. Her subconscious had imprinted a painful message, "You're not enough. You don't belong." And that emotional imprint had stayed with her ever since.

I then asked her subconscious to guide us to a Subsequent Sensitizing Event, another time in her life when she felt the same way.

"How old are you now?"

"Seven. I'm on the playground."

"What's happening?"

"The other kids are laughing at me again."

"Why?"

"Because of my shirt," she said, visibly uncomfortable.

"Tell me more."

"One of the girls in class used to own this shirt. Her mom do-

The Unconscious **Authority**

nated it to Goodwill. My mom bought it there... and now her daughter told everyone it was hers. She pointed at me and said, 'That used to be mine!'"

Her voice cracked, "Now everyone's laughing. Again."

These weren't isolated incidents. They were evidence, building a case in her subconscious, forming a false but deeply felt belief... I'm less than. I'm not good enough. I'll be rejected if I try to stand out.

This belief, buried for decades, had become her internal compass, and it was pointing away from the Postmaster job. Not because she couldn't handle it, but because her subconscious was trying to protect her from the humiliation and rejection it remembered so vividly from childhood.

The subconscious can't tell the difference between past and present. It doesn't reason or analyze. It simply reacts to emotional patterns. When Cindy thought about her new position, her reticular activating system, the brain's emotional filter, scanned her memory bank and unconsciously lit up all the old times she had felt "less than." As a result, her UA threw up emotional roadblocks, anxiety, insomnia, and dread. Its job was to keep her safe. But in doing so, it was also keeping her small.

As we continued the session, we uncovered several more memories with the same emotional fingerprint. Moments of rejection, embarrassment, and emotional abandonment that reinforced her unconscious story.

But now that these events were finally being seen for what they were. Painful, yes, but also misinterpreted by a young child, Cindy could start letting them go. She released them one by one, each memory losing its emotional charge.

I guided her to speak to her younger self — the little girl playing with the single Barbie, the seven-year-old in the hand-me-down shirt.

"Tell her what she needed to hear."

She whispered, "You are enough. You are smart, and kind, and worthy. What happened wasn't your fault. Those kids didn't know any better... but I do."

That was the turning point.

She came out of the session lighter — softer around the eyes, more grounded in her body. A few days later, she called me and said, "I cried all the way home. But they weren't sad tears. I felt like something finally left me — like I'd been holding it in for years."

Her subconscious had finally released the outdated programming. The Unconscious Authority no longer had to guard her from a threat that wasn't there anymore.

Cindy stepped into her role as Postmaster with calm, clarity, and earned confidence. She served her community well until she eventually retired — not from fear, but with pride.

Today, Cindy volunteers with senior citizens in her hometown,

The Unconscious **Authority**

lending her time and wisdom freely, without fear of judgment or inadequacy. She doesn't need to prove anything anymore.

She knows she's enough.

The Trainer and the Nasty Stepmother

Mike looked like a walking fitness poster when he stepped into my office, broad shoulders, muscled arms, and a confident stride. He owned a successful health club and had spent most of his life in the gym. This guy knew his stuff. But as he sat down, I noticed something odd... in one hand, a half-eaten protein bar; in the other, a blender bottle filled with some sort of chalky-looking health shake.

After a little casual conversation, I asked him about the shake-and-bar combo. His response came quickly, like he'd said it a hundred times, "It's about all I can eat. Otherwise, I'll bloat up like a toad."

I raised an eyebrow.

"So what do you want to eat?" I asked.

"Oh, I love food. I enjoy just about everything... but I can't eat like a normal person and maintain my weight," he replied.

"It all goes to my gut."

Now here's the thing, Mike wasn't overweight by any traditional standard. He was actually very well-proportioned. But to him, there was always this stubborn layer of fat clinging to his midsection — a shield that blocked the sculpted abs he worked so hard to earn.

"I can't lose it," he said with frustration.

"I work out constantly, I avoid bad foods, and I coach other people through their transformations. They drop pounds like crazy — but my belly fat won't budge."

It was like he was living a double life, expert trainer to his clients, but prisoner to his own body.

What happened next surprised even him. Mike had one hypnosis session, and within a week he called me, absolutely lit up with the news... "You're not gonna believe this, the weight's falling off like crazy! And I'm eating actual food again!"

Now, let's pause for a second. This wasn't about a new diet, workout routine, or miracle supplement. Mike already had access to all of that. He owned the gym. He was the guy with the answers. So why had his own body defied every logical effort?

Because logic wasn't running the show. His Unconscious Authority was.

In his session, once Mike was in a deeply relaxed state, I asked his subconscious mind to speak up, "What emotion is behind this weight?"

Without hesitation, Mike's body tensed, and he shouted, "Anger!"

We had struck the nerve. This wasn't about fat or fitness, it was about *emotional insulation*.

The Unconscious **Authority**

I directed his subconscious to take us back to the first time he ever felt that anger. His mind didn't go to a gym, or a dinner table, or a mirror. It went to his childhood.

He regressed to a memory where he was eight or nine years old.

"Where are you?" I asked.

"In my house... my stepmom's yelling at me."

"What's happening?"

"She just called me a 'worthless little bastard.'"

His jaw clenched. His voice cracked.

"She said it in front of my dad. He didn't say anything. I hate her for it, but I don't want to cause problems."

That one moment — that string of careless, cruel words — left a bigger mark than anything in the gym ever could. And it wasn't just a one-time thing. Her verbal jabs were regular, often disguised as "tough love," but they stung all the same. Deep down, Mike despised her behavior, but he loved his father too much to rock the boat. So he buried it. Never confronted it. Never processed it. Just absorbed it.

And what did the Unconscious Authority do with that message?

It built a shield.... *a belly*.

A subtle, physical barrier between Mike and the ideal version of himself. Because if he ever really looked like the lean, confident, powerful man he wanted to be — if he ever became too visible, too successful, too confident — he might open himself up to more pain, more ridicule, more "worthless" labels.

That layer of fat was *armor*.

The UA doesn't care about your limited diet or protein intake. It cares about protecting you, even if that protection is completely outdated.

Once that memory was revisited and processed, and Mike saw that those words were never true, but just projections of an insecure woman who had no business speaking to a child that way — his mind finally let go. The UA released its grip.

He forgave the past. He updated the story. And his body followed suit.

From that point on, Mike's weight stabilized. His midsection leaned out. His abs became fully visible. And he didn't have to live on shakes and protein bars anymore. He started eating real food again, enjoying dinners with friends and even the occasional indulgence, without guilt or consequence.

Why? Because the story had changed.

Before, he was unconsciously living as the "worthless little bastard," unable to fully own the image of success he helped others achieve. After the session, he became Mike — trainer, business owner, and fully integrated man with a six-pack to prove it.

That's the power of the Unconscious Authority.

Today, Mike continues to train clients, eats like a human being, and walks around with the body he always dreamed of — not because he changed his diet, but because he changed his mind.

The Teacher Crush and Fear of Girls

Tim was a 34-year-old guy with a challenge that made absolutely no sense to him and honestly, from the outside, it didn't make sense to me either.

When he came to my office, he said something right out of the gate that set the tone...

"Joe, I'm truly perplexed. I like ladies. I enjoy talking to them... but I just can't approach them. When I think about walking up to a woman and starting a conversation, I feel extreme anxiety. I don't know what to do."

Now, this wasn't some shy, awkward, pimple-faced teenager. Tim was a good-looking, articulate guy with solid confidence in most areas of his life, especially at work and in his hobbies. He had friends. He had a life. But when it came to women? His brain hit the panic button.

Naturally, I knew the conscious mind wasn't the culprit here. This had subconscious protection mechanism written all over it. So I placed Tim into a deeply relaxed state, and we got to work using regression therapy, guiding his subconscious to take us back to the very first scene, situation, or event that had everything to do with this mysterious anxiety around women.

"Where are you?" I asked.

Joe **Hammer**

"I'm in school."

"What grade are you in?"

"Fourth grade."

"Tell me what's going on."

"I have a crush on my teacher... but I don't think she likes me anymore."

His voice softened.

"Why do you think that?"

"Because she made me sit in the corner for talking during class. All the other kids are laughing at me."

Boom.

The "love of his life" — or at least his childhood version of her — had just publicly rejected and humiliated him. To a fourth grader, being sent to the corner wasn't just punishment. It was a signal... *you're not wanted.* And when you're in elementary school with an unchecked imagination and a wide-open heart, your teacher isn't just a teacher — she's your future wife, your first love, your everything.

Now, we as adults know that a kid having a crush on a teacher isn't going anywhere. But Tim's critical faculty — the part of the mind that separates fantasy from reality — wasn't fully developed back then. He really thought he had a "shot." So, when she singled him out and embarrassed him, it left a deep emotional bruise.

The Unconscious **Authority**

I then asked his subconscious to move us to the next event — the Subsequent Sensitizing Event (SSE), another moment that reinforced this developing belief that girls didn't like him.

"Where are you now?" I asked.

"I'm on the playground."

"What's going on?"

"I really like Marsha and want her to be my girlfriend. We're all playing... but the other kids are laughing at my shirt."

"Why are they laughing?"

"Marsha says it looks like I'm wearing pajamas."

Another crush, another emotional jab, this time from the girl he liked.

Innocent? Sure. Cruel? Maybe not. But to Tim's young subconscious, it was more proof that "girls make fun of me." The story was building.

Then came the next memory, a middle school dance. He mustered the courage to ask a girl to go with him. She said yes. Progress, right?

But the day before the dance?

"She cancelled," he said. "She went with another guy instead."

Strike three. Different age, different girl — same feeling of rejection. And this time, it stung even more.

Joe **Hammer**

As these little heartbreaks piled up, Tim's Unconscious Authority — that inner security system whose only job is to protect us — took action. It didn't understand context or intention. It didn't know that kids can be thoughtless or that people change. All it knew was... "Women are dangerous. Every time you open your heart, they hurt you. Let's not let that happen anymore."

And so, it built a wall. A subconscious protection system. Every time Tim even thought about approaching a woman, the UA jumped in, "Nope! Not safe!"

Cue anxiety. Sweaty palms. Racing heart. Abort mission.

It worked perfectly and kept him safe from new hurt. But it also kept him single, lonely, and frustrated.

So, during our session, I did what any good subconscious negotiator would do, I had a heart-to-heart with that part of him that had been trying to protect him for decades.

We acknowledged the past. We thanked it for doing its job. And then, we gave it permission to let go... to stop protecting the man from the outdated fears of the boy.

The old beliefs — "Girls will laugh at me," "They don't want me," "I'm not good enough" — were gently released. And we replaced them with something much more honest and helpful.

Tim came out of the session feeling lighter, like he'd just let go of a thousand pounds of emotional baggage. But I didn't want that new energy to sit idle. So I gave him a little assignment.

"I want you to go to the mall," I told him, "and talk to as many

The Unconscious **Authority**

women as you can. Just simple conversations. Nothing heavy. No pickup lines. Just connect."

He called me the next day, buzzing with excitement.

"Joe, I spent three hours at the mall yesterday — and I talked to everybody! Not only was it easy, but I got a coffee date for this weekend!"

Ba da bing.

Today, Tim is dating, confident, and no longer ruled by the echoes of a teacher's punishment or a playground insult. He no longer sees women as danger zones — just people, like him, looking to connect!

The "Drag" and the Chronic Cough

Sherry initially came to see me for help with weight control. But as we began our pre-session chat, I couldn't help but notice something unusual.

She kept coughing. Not the occasional throat-clearing kind of cough, I'm talking deep, sharp, almost body-shaking coughs. The kind that makes you think, she is coming down with something.

So I asked the obvious question:

"Do you have a cold?"

"No," she said, "I always cough when I'm nervous or stressed."

I found that interesting.

Joe **Hammer**

"Tell me more about that," I probed.

"Well, I'm a hairstylist. I'm around chemicals and hairspray all the time. I think that's part of it."

Ah, the conscious mind's rational explanation. Logical. Convenient. Also... not the real reason.

As you've learned, the conscious mind is great at making up stories that sound true but usually aren't. It loves to assign meaning and slap a "That's probably it" sticker on experiences that are actually rooted far deeper.

So I pushed a little further.

"Okay, but what do hairstyling chemicals have to do with coughing when you're stressed?" I asked. "There aren't any chemicals in this office."

She paused and thought about it.

I added, "This cough is going to interfere with your session. We can work on the weight issue, but we've got to get this handled first — it's clearly not just about hairspray."

Something clicked. She agreed.

And so, we shifted focus. Sherry decided to use her session to explore this mysterious, long-running "stress cough" — something she had simply gotten used to over the years, like a background noise in her life.

I placed her into a relaxed state and guided her subconscious

The Unconscious **Authority**

mind to take us back to the Initial Sensitizing Event — the very first moment this cough took root.

"Where are you?" I asked.

"I'm on the drag."

"The what?"

I had no idea what she meant — "on the drag"? I kept going.

"Tell me what's happening."

Suddenly, her tone changed.

"There's dirt in my mouth! There's dirt in my mouth!"

And with that, she started coughing violently.

It was so intense, I slid the office trashcan beside her chair. For a moment, I genuinely thought she might vomit.

After calming things down, we kept going. Her subconscious started filling in the blanks.

Sherry was three years old. Her father worked at a racetrack. Between horse races, they would smooth the dirt surface of the track by pulling a makeshift drag — basically a heavy section of chain-link fence, weighed down with railroad ties and cement blocks — to flatten the hoof divots left behind.

The drag was pulled by a tractor. And for kids, it was a ride. A bumpy, dusty, exciting ride on top of this contraption.

That day, her father was driving the tractor. Sherry and a few of

Joe **Hammer**

her little friends were sitting on the drag. But during the slow ride, something went wrong.

She shifted position and unknowingly placed her foot beneath the front edge of the drag. It caught her and yanked her downward. She fell face-first into the soft dirt and was pulled under the weighted section of fencing.

By some miracle, she wasn't physically hurt — the weight of the drag was distributed over a wide area. But her face hit the earth and she got a full mouthful of dirt.

Her friends screamed. Her father stopped the tractor. And when he saw what happened, he didn't rush over to hug her. He didn't comfort her.

He yelled at her.

He chastised her for being "foolish," for putting her foot in the wrong place — all while she stood there coughing, crying, and spitting dirt in front of a growing crowd of spectators from the grandstands.

"There were so many people staring at me," she recalled in the session, "just... staring at my dirty face. I thought I was going to die."

Shame. Embarrassment. Fear. Physical distress. All wrapped up in one unforgettable moment.

And it was in that moment that her Unconscious Authority connected the dots... "When you're scared and overwhelmed, you cough."

The Unconscious **Authority**

The cough had nothing to do with hairspray.

It was an emotional reflex, hardwired from a childhood trauma that had never fully resolved. Her subconscious had stored that moment, and every time her nervous system detected a similar "threat" — even a small one — it triggered the coughing as if to remove the "dirt" again. It was trying to keep her safe in the only way it knew how.

For decades, Sherry's adult life was peppered with stress-induced coughing fits she couldn't explain. But after the session?

Gone.

The deep subconscious association was brought to the surface, examined, and cleared. And once the mind no longer needed that old protection pattern, it let it go.

Afterward, Sherry told me, "I remembered that situation, but never thought of it as that big of a deal."

"It most often never is," I replied.

That's the nature of the Unconscious Authority. It doesn't operate on logic. It operates on emotional impact. Even moments we'd consider "small" can become the blueprint for lifelong behavior when they hit us hard enough — especially when we're kids.

Today, Sherry no longer coughs when she's stressed. No matter what life throws at her — salon drama, traffic, family — she handles it without the body's old reflex kicking in. She's free from that dusty little loop that started on a racetrack decades ago.

Joe **Hammer**

The Roofer and the After Dark Panic Attacks

Tom came to see me for one simple reason, he wanted to sleep. Specifically, he wanted to sleep without having nightly panic attacks — the kind that pulled him out of bed, jolted his heart rate, and left him sitting in front of a box fan at 3 a.m. trying to remember how to breathe.

He'd recently gotten married and was now a stepdad. He wanted to enjoy that new chapter in life. But every night, like clockwork, anxiety would grip him the moment he tried to relax. The idea of falling asleep? Terrifying.

He was on several medications for anxiety and panic disorders, but his doctor agreed to pause them temporarily so Tom could try a different route... regression-based hypnotherapy.

During his session, Tom relived the moment that changed his life.

He had been a construction worker, doing a routine roofing job. One misstep sent him plummeting off the roof. He blacked out on impact.

The next thing he remembered was waking up in a hospital bed. In the dark. No idea where he was.

And worse? He couldn't feel his legs.

"I can't feel my legs!" he shouted, reliving the moment.

He told me how he screamed for help and how a nurse came in and tried to calm him down. She explained the situation, but all he could focus on was the terrifying possibility that he might

The Unconscious **Authority**

never walk again.

Eventually, he regained sensation. With time and therapy, most of his physical strength returned. But the emotional damage — the imprint that experience left behind — was still very much alive.

And that's the thing about trauma... the body may heal, but the Unconscious Authority remembers.

Continuing the hypnosis session, I guided Tom into a relaxed state and directed his subconscious to return to the moment that had emotionally installed this panic response, the scene where everything changed.

Sure enough, we landed right back in that hospital room.

He was flat on his back. It was dark. He was alone. He was scared.

And that position, lying down in the dark, became forever linked to panic. His subconscious had made a note... This position equals danger. This moment equals terror. Don't fall asleep in this state. Stay alert.

So every night in his normal bed, decades later, the UA stepped in to "protect" him — by triggering panic attacks.

Don't let him relax. Don't let him lie there motionless. Get him up. Get him out of bed. Keep him alive.

That's how the subconscious works. It doesn't care about logic. It's not checking to see if you're safe now. It just remembers when you weren't.

Once we uncovered that connection and, more importantly, once his subconscious accepted that the danger had passed, that his body had healed, and there was no longer any need to sound the nightly alarm, it let go of the panic mechanism.

And the results were immediate.

Tom returned to normal sleep patterns. No more fan therapy at midnight. No more sudden jolts of anxiety just for trying to go to bed. And in the weeks following our session, he was weaned off his anxiety medications with his doctor's supervision.

He got his nights back.

He got his peace back.

And maybe best of all — he got to enjoy his new family the way he always wanted to, fully present, fully awake... and fully rested!

"Oh, That's Just Bethany..."

Bethany came to see me after life had thrown her a few curveballs—a tough divorce, a once-compulsive shopping habit (which she'd heroically wrestled into submission with the help of Debtors Anonymous), and now a new relationship on the horizon. From the outside, things looked pretty okay. But inside? Not so much.

When she filled out her intake form, she referenced one central theme: money and self-worth. She suspected her challenges weren't just logistical or circumstantial, but psychological; rooted in those old, half-forgotten childhood messages that take

The Unconscious **Authority**

root when you're too young to question them and grow into full-blown belief systems by adulthood.

In her own words, Bethany said she struggled with "not believing in herself." And she didn't just say it—she felt it, in every area of her life.

She listed off her emotional cocktail on the form like a sad menu... anxious, guilty, unloved, inadequate, confused, fearful, obsessive. Basically, a sampler platter of subconscious distress.

One prompt on the intake asked her to recall any repeated phrases from childhood. She wrote: "Oh, that's just Bethany. She's so different."

And the classic, "Money doesn't grow on trees."

Innocent as they may sound, phrases like those are the emotional termites of the psyche... quiet, sneaky, and capable of doing major structural damage over time.

Bethany didn't grow up in a house full of rage or chaos. But what she did grow up with was worse in some ways... emotional absence. A perpetually unhappy father and a mother who was there, but not there. The kind of upbringing that silently whispers to a child, "You're on your own. You'll have to work to be noticed. To be loved. To matter."

Her first regression session surfaced some major insights. We didn't quite crack the whole code (yet), but one thing stood out loud and clear, a family phrase, *"Oh, that's just Bethany..."* had been adopted as a default defense mechanism by her Unconscious Authority. It gave her unspoken permission to expect rejection. And to react to even the possibility of dismissal with all the emotional force of a five-alarm fire.

Enter Bill.

Bill was her new partner. Kind-hearted. Grounded. Thoughtful. He genuinely adored Bethany. They had a few rocky moments in their relationship, but overall things were progressing.

Until they weren't.

During a dinner date, Bethany casually dropped the bomb that she and her ex-husband had been thinking about reconciling. Naturally, Bill was caught off guard. Still, he respected her honesty and chose to give her space. Later, when she reassured him the ex was officially out of the picture, Bill cautiously opened the door again.

They eventually made a little pinky-swear pact to leave past mistakes they had both made behind them and start fresh.

Things were good.

Until they weren't.

Bethany began reacting to some common situations with intensity. Bill would make an offhand comment and she'd shoot back, "I don't know how I should take that." That's emotional hypervigilance, when you're not just listening to what someone says, but scanning for hidden danger beneath their words.

He'd try to clarify, but she'd shut down. It wasn't just emotion-

The Unconscious **Authority**

al, it was disproportionate.

This is what psychologists call *emotional flooding,* often rooted in old attachment wounds. And in Bethany's case, her Unconscious Authority was running a familiar tape:

"Here comes the rejection. Just like before."

Take Easter Sunday. They'd planned a fun egg hunt for her kids. After church, Bill stayed behind to help the minister and fellow congregants set up brunch tables. He texted Bethany to let her know he'd be 30 minutes late.

Her response? Full meltdown.

"You don't care about us. You always put us second."

Tears. Frustration. Emotional collapse.

Meanwhile, the kids were chilling. Watching cartoons. Not a single egg was harmed in the making of the holiday event.

But that's how subconscious protection works—it doesn't react to what's happening. It reacts to what *once happened*. To what it thinks is happening. In this case, it wasn't about an egg hunt or a text message. It was about a little girl who waited, emotionally and literally, for someone to show up. And who, somewhere along the way, made an unconscious vow... "Never again will I be second."

Now, let's talk sneakers.

Before meeting Bill, Bethany had dreamed up her own line of

Joe Hammer

stylish high-end, all-natural, ethically sourced designer sneakers, with a $300 price tag.

She'd already started ordering inventory when she asked Bill, who was a recognized and experienced marketing consultant, for his feedback.

He appreciated the vision but gently pointed out the logistical hurdles, such as high capital needs, inventory management, anticipated dilemmas with overseas manufacturing, and, most importantly, the fact that even Nike had failed at launching a similar natural-materials line.

His intention was to be helpful. Grounding. Strategic. After all, that was Bill's area of expertise.

But Bethany didn't hear insight, she heard *doubt*.

She pushed back. "Every major brand started small," she argued. And while she wasn't wrong, this wasn't a conversation about facts. It was a conversation about feelings. Her Unconscious Authority didn't hear "market research." It heard, "You don't believe in me."

In that moment, Bill realized this wasn't about sneakers or business models. It was about old wounds dressed up as entrepreneurial ambition. Accepting his advice would have meant questioning herself, and that was off-limits.

Bethany wasn't rejecting Bill's feedback because it lacked merit. She was rejecting it because accepting it would have confirmed her deepest fear… "I'm not enough."

The Unconscious **Authority**

So, Bill backed off. Kindly. Quietly. He could see where this was going.

Fast-forward a few months. Bethany invites Bill to join her and the kids at a water park—or, if he's busy, to just meet them later for dinner.

Bill chooses dinner. Work stuff.

Bethany's reaction? Same script, different day.

"You always put us second."

Never mind that he picked one of the two options she gave him. Her UA wasn't tracking logic. It was tracking abandonment. It heard, once again, "He didn't choose me."

Bethany ended the relationship at that point and became avoidant... not because of a water park or an Easter brunch or even advice about her sneakers, but because her UA was trying to protect her from something it didn't realize was no longer a threat... rejection, dismissal, emotional invisibility.

So what was really going on?

Sure, it's possible Bethany was still emotionally entangled with her ex and unconsciously sabotaging the new relationship. But more likely it was was childhood trauma echoing through adult circumstances.

Her UA had internalized the belief, "You're not a priority." And now, every emotionally charged situation lit up that same old neural pathway. Different context. Same conclusion.

Joe **Hammer**

Bethany's Unconscious Authority wasn't the villain in her story. It was the guard dog—barking at every shadow, convinced a threat was near just because once, there was one.

What Bethany needs now isn't another business plan or relationship. It's a map back to those early moments when her identity was shaped by subtle, forgettable comments that added up to those persistent beliefs...

You're different. You don't fit. You're not enough.

Until those original imprints are identified and reprocessed, she'll keep playing out the same script—with different cast members, same storyline.

Many people who've faced rejection spend their lives chasing validation—whether through people, achievements, or titles that prop up their self-worth or hide deeper insecurities. In Bethany's case, that meant earning a "doctorate" from a diploma mill—a school with no real accreditation or academic standing. While it may have felt like an accomplishment, the truth is, credentials from these kinds of institutions do more harm than good. They don't boost credibility—they damage it. Instead of being a mark of expertise, they're often just ego bandages disguised as degrees.

And as for that sneaker line? Who knows. Given the market realities, it's unlikely they'll be a breakout success. But that's not the real story here. The real story is that quiet voice inside—the one that still whispers, "You're not worth choosing."

The Unconscious **Authority**

Bethany's story isn't over. Not by a long shot. But with any luck her time with Bill gave her something valuable... a mirror. A magnifying glass. A chance to see that her strongest emotional reactions weren't about what was happening now... they were about what happened *then*.

That's the power of the Unconscious Authority. So, if you've ever caught yourself saying, "I don't know why I reacted that way," or "I guess that's just how I am," take a beat. That might not be the real you talking... it might just be your inner Bethany!

The Lifelong Stutterer

Jerry was in his 40s, and had stuttered for as long as he could remember. It wasn't just a minor speech hiccup—it was a full-body event. The more anxious he felt, the more his words locked up.

He'd tried everything. And I mean everything.

Speech therapists? Dozens.

Breathing exercises? Check.

Metronome therapy? Yep—he'd practiced speaking in rhythm like he was narrating a poem.

Delayed auditory feedback headset? He spent $500 on one that made him sound like a robot.

Reading aloud every day? Tried it.

Joe **Hammer**

Mirror work? Yep.

He even did a public speaking course that made him more nervous than the stutter itself.

He could probably teach a graduate-level course on stuttering interventions.

But nothing stuck.

People told him to slow down.

Breathe.

Think before you speak.

All well-meaning, all useless.

One day, a friend suggested hypnosis.

Jerry laughed out loud.

"Hypnosis? Why, so I stutter while clucking like a chicken?"

Still, there must've been a quiet whisper of curiosity under the sarcasm, because he made the call. He admitted later he booked the appointment mostly just to "prove it wouldn't work."

Our first session took longer than most. His stutter was in full stress mode, and every sentence was a wrestling match. But I wasn't in a rush. The subconscious doesn't work on a stopwatch.

Once he felt safe, we eased into regression work.

I asked his subconscious to bring up the ISE, the original

The Unconscious **Authority**

event... the moment when the stutter took root. Not just the symptoms, but the seed.

Almost immediately, he was there.

"I'm getting a beating from my dad," he said, his voice now steady within trance.

"He won't let me cry. He keeps saying, 'Be a man. Take your punishment.'"

I asked gently, "Is this the first time it happened?"

"No," he replied.

"He does it all the time."

His young mind had learned early on that showing emotion was dangerous. Tears were weakness. Crying invited more punishment.

But here's the thing, when a child can't cry, can't scream, can't say help—the body finds another way to hold it all in. In Jerry's case it was the stutter.

It wasn't a speech issue. It was an emotional traffic jam. His words had to squeeze through the same bottleneck that once tried to suppress his screams.

There it was, the frozen grief. The swallowed cries. The unspoken terror.

The stutter wasn't random—it was a protective mechanism.

We worked through each of those memories. One by one, like

peeling old wallpaper off the walls of his mind.

We explored not just what happened—but why his dad behaved that way. Jerry realized his father had never been taught how to parent with patience. He was a product of his own pain, passing down what he learned from his father.

We then moved into forgiveness work. The deep, gritty kind. We released the shame, the fear, the belief that it was somehow his fault.

We told the subconscious:

It's safe now.

You're allowed to speak.

You're allowed to feel.

You don't need to hold it all in anymore.

And then, slowly, we emerged from trance.

Jerry looked at me like a kid seeing snow for the first time.

"Wow."

I didn't want to push him to speak too quickly, but I was dying to see if the stutter had shifted. I looked around for something he could read—no books, no magazines. So I handed him his intake form and pointed to the disclaimer at the bottom.

"Read this out loud."

He nodded, still wiping tears from the corner of his eyes.

The Unconscious **Authority**

And then… he read the whole thing.

Fluently. Clearly.

Not a single stutter.

When he finished, he looked up with wide, blinking eyes.

"Is it gone?" he asked.

I smiled.

Even though I wasn't certain, I responded, "Sure is."

And it was.

That lifelong struggle—that daily reminder of unprocessed pain—was gone.

It wasn't about retraining his speech patterns, it was about releasing what had silenced him in the first place.

Jerry walked out of that office with a lighter step, like someone had finally loosened the emotional tourniquet around his throat.

He didn't just gain his voice back. He gained permission to feel.

That's the power of the subconscious.

Jerry's stutter wasn't who he was, it was who he had to become to survive.

And once survival wasn't the goal anymore—once freedom became the goal—his voice returned home!

Joe **Hammer**

The Trucker's Enduring Back Pain

I hesitated to put this case in the first edition of this book. Why? Because it deals with something that's often lumped into the "woo-woo" bin of healing modalities... *past life regression.*

Back when I was completing my hypnosis certification, I saw it listed in the curriculum. My immediate reaction?

"Yeah... I'll be skipping that part, thanks."

To me, past life regression was right up there with tarot cards and late-night psychic hotlines. I'd seen enough cringey ads from questionable "hypnotists" promising to reveal your royal Egyptian lineage or alien abduction saga. Hard pass.

So I approached my instructor and politely asked if I could skip that portion of the training. He emphatically declined.

"You don't understand it yet," he said, "but after you go through it, you'll be glad you did."

I wasn't a happy camper. Now I had to sit through a section I didn't believe in? Ugh. But I stuck it out.

To my surprise, I actually learned a lot, especially about the process and how, belief aside, it could be used as a powerful metaphorical tool for healing. Still, I had no plans to offer "discover-who-you-were-in-a-past-life" sessions anytime soon.

Then came Ed.

Ed was a trucker. Big guy. Barrel chest. Wore a ballcap. And

The Unconscious **Authority**

he'd been dealing with chronic lower back pain for decades. He'd tried everything.

Chiropractors

Acupuncture

Physical therapy

Massage therapy

Ice packs, heating pads, lumbar supports, inversion tables

CBD creams, Tiger Balm, Essential Oils

Foam rolling

Yoga (he left halfway through the first class when asked to "breathe into his tailbone")

He even got his truck's driver seat upgraded. "It's like sitting on a cloud," he said. "More comfortable than my La-Z-Boy."

And of course, he was on a steady diet of Tylenol—his breakfast, lunch, and sometimes dinner buddy.

The kicker? Multiple MRIs, X-rays, and tests showed nothing wrong. No herniated discs, no visible spinal issues, no postural imbalances.

His doctor finally threw his hands up and called me.

"Joe," he said, "you helped my brother out of a dark place. Maybe you can help Ed. We're out of answers. He's got real pain, but no one can find a cause."

Joe **Hammer**

I agreed... as long as Ed was open to the process and not just doing it because his doc "told him to."

A few weeks later, Ed showed up at my office. We spent some time chatting about his life, his work, his long hours behind the wheel. Nothing unusual came up. His back didn't hurt more when he drove or sat—it was just always there.

"Ever injured your back?" I asked.

"Nope. Played sports in high school, but never took a hard hit or fall," he replied.

So, with nothing obvious presenting in his current life, I guided him into trance and gave a simple suggestion to his subconscious, "Take us back to this back pain—the first time it showed up, regardless of time or space."

Ed began to shift and squirm in his chair. His face contorted as if he were reliving something intense.

"On a scale of 1 to 10, what's the pain level?"

"Ten," he barked, almost reflexively.

"Where are you?" I asked.

"Outside," he said through clenched teeth.

"Are you alone or with others?"

He paused... "There are others... but I don't know them."

"The horses! The horses! They're going to trample me!" he shouted, as his arms instinctively shot up to shield his body.

The Unconscious **Authority**

Okay... now I was the one squirming.

"Are there people on the horses?" I asked.

"Yes!"

"Do you recognize them?"

"No... they're wearing armor."

Armor?! I'm thinking, what is this, Gladiator?

"What's around you?"

"Sand. Just sand."

"And your back?"

"There's a... a... *spear* in my back!"

Boom. There it was.

I immediately flashed back to my training—when in doubt, don't debate, just clean it up.

I told him to imagine the warriors and horses fading away. Then I guided him through removing the spear—slowly, gently, painlessly. I had him visualize golden healing light pouring into the wound, mending it with warmth and strength. The sand dried. The sun shone. His breath slowed.

"What's your pain level now?"

"It's a two," he said, visibly calmer.

We did a bit more work, and by the end of the session, he said it was a one.

Joe **Hammer**

I brought him out of trance, and he looked at me like he'd just seen an alien from another galaxy.

"What the hell was that?" he asked.

Whether it was a real past life, a dream from childhood, or something the subconscious pulled from an old movie—his nervous system treated it like it was real. The emotion, the trauma, the imagery—it all stuck. And the unconscious mind has been guarding that spot ever since.

And just like that, his pain was gone.

He walked out straighter, lighter—and hasn't needed Tylenol since.

Now, was it truly a past life? Maybe.

Could it have been a childhood dream inspired by Ben-Hur, 300, Excalibur, or some other medieval movie he may have watched with his parents? Absolutely.

Does it matter? Not really.

The subconscious latched onto that image—whether fact, fiction, or fantasy—and encoded it as a threat. That's what it does. It's protective. Sometimes overly so.

Author and psychiatrist Brian Weiss, one of the pioneers of past life regression, shares in his book, *Many Lives, Many Masters* how unresolved past-life trauma can carry forward, affecting us in the present. Whether you believe in literal reincarnation or see it as metaphor, the healing is real. And that's what matters.

The Unconscious **Authority**

Ed is pain-free today. He's still driving trucks. And he still swears that cloud-seat is the second most comfortable thing he's ever experienced... the first was getting that damn spear out of his back.

So if your body's hurting and no one can figure out why, maybe it's time to look a little deeper... *or farther back.*

The Persistent Pimples

Kristina came to my office for hypnosis—because of *pimples*.

Yep, you read that right. Not trauma. Not public speaking anxiety. Not even quitting vaping. She wanted to know why her acne was still hanging around, ten years past puberty.

"It doesn't make sense," she said. "I eat clean. I don't drink. I wash my face religiously. What gives?"

She was frustrated. Her skin-care routine read like a pharmaceutical thesis. She'd already tried:

Every over-the-counter wash from Neutrogena.

Dermatologist-prescribed topicals that could likely dissolve concrete. Antibiotics. Probiotics to rebuild the what the antibiotics took away. Going dairy-free, gluten-free, sugar-free, joy-free. Red light therapy. Jade rollers.

Even monthly facials with extractions that felt more like medieval torture

At one point, she even tried manifesting clear skin by saying affirmations to her pores. "I radiate cleanliness and confidence," she whispered into her mirror. Her zits were unimpressed.

So when she showed up asking for hypnosis, I didn't flinch. Stranger things have healed stranger ailments.

We began by talking through every possible reason her conscious mind could invent for the acne… hormones, stress, maybe repressed rage against almond milk? But ultimately, we landed on the sacred, humbling diagnosis… "I don't know."

Perfect. That meant it was time to go deeper.

I guided Kristina into trance and regressed her to the initial sensitizing event—the very first time her subconscious connected to this skin issue.

"Where are you?" I asked.

"I'm 5 and I'm in bed with my mom and dad."

"What's happening?"

"When I wake up, I always go into their room and cuddle with them…" Her voice softened. Her face twitched and a tiny tear emerged.

"What's going on?"

"Daddy's teasing me. He says my breath stinks. He calls me… 'dog breath.'"

Yikes. There it was. A tiny but emotionally loaded moment.

"Is that the first time he said it?"

The Unconscious **Authority**

"No... he says it every morning. It makes me sad."

Now, I know what you're thinking, "What does morning breath have to do with acne?" Well Grasshopper, welcome to the funhouse called the subconscious mind.

It doesn't operate by logical rules. It speaks in metaphor, emotion, and sticky little moments like this one.

To little Kristina, being told her breath stank, repeatedly, by someone she loved and trusted, became a moment of shame and emotional rejection. A child's unconscious can't rationalize adult sarcasm. It just feels the sting. And sometimes, that emotional sting burrows in and pops back out in unexpected ways... like a breakout of zits.

We went through a forgiveness process. Kristina, in trance, told her dad how those words had made her feel. She expressed the sadness, the confusion, the hurt. And then she let it go.

She forgave him for the unintentional harm because, let's be honest, most "dog breath" comments are issued with dad-level goofiness, not cruelty.

Then I helped her reframe that old memory with love and protection—imagining her five-year-old self being comforted, reassured, and told, "You're beautiful. You're safe. Your body is safe. You are loved just as you are."

She emerged from trance looking lighter. She blinked, sipped water, and said,

"That was... weird. But I feel kind of amazing."

A few days later, she emailed me.

"You're not going to believe this, but my skin is clearing up. Like... noticeably. Even my esthetician said, 'What are you doing differently?' I told her, 'Apparently, forgiving my dad.'"

And just like that, her persistent pimples went poof.

Now, was it really the teasing that caused her acne? Maybe. Maybe not. The truth is, we don't always get clean answers. The subconscious is more like a poet than a scientist.

But here's what I know, when we release old emotional residue, the body often follows suit.

Kristina got her answer.

After hearing of her healing, her dad sent her a giant bouquet of flowers with a card that said, "Sorry about the dog breath thing. You've always been beautiful, and I love you with all my heart."

I'd call that a clear win – and without Clearasil!

That's Illogical Captain!

What do I find most interesting about these cases?

Well, if you're looking for logic—don't.

One thing becomes immediately clear as you dig through the layers of human behavior and memory... the Unconscious Authority doesn't care about logic. It doesn't care about facts, data, or adult-level rationality. It's not Spock. It's not even Kirk. It's more like a slightly panicked security guard watching over your stuff.

The Unconscious Authority

There was no viable reason for the UA to keep these clients stuck in protective mode based on their experiences from the past. And yet, there it was—like a stubborn old dog barking at the mailman just in case he turns out to be a threat this time.

It makes no sense... and that's the point.

The Subconscious is the World's Most Over-Protective Friend

The subconscious is a brilliant, loyal, and often comically over-reactive part of us. It's constantly working to keep us alive, safe, and pain-free. But here's the catch... *it has zero reasoning capability. None. Nada.*

So instead of weighing pros and cons, it clings to old, emotionally charged data and says, "the last time we felt this way, it didn't go well. Let's never feel this way again. Activate defenses! Call in the zits, back pain, anxiety attacks—whatever gets the job done!"

If that sounds ridiculous, it's because it is. And yet, this is exactly how many deep-seated issues form.

Think about it... when you look at what originally caused and then later triggered the challenges these individuals experienced, it's never anything heavy. It's usually something deceptively simple. A teasing comment. A forgotten childhood memory.

Things that, in the adult world, are most often shrugged off in seconds—but in the subconscious world, they're catalogued as

DEFCON 1 events and stored in the permanent archive.

That's because the subconscious doesn't understand time either. It lives in the eternal present. So if something hurt you once, even decades ago, it might still be protecting you from it today, as though the event is still happening.

It's easy to look back and say, "Why would anyone's mind do this to them?"

As you have learned, the subconscious doesn't reason. it reacts. It's not interested in what's fair or logical—it only wants to avoid pain and repeat pleasure.

It doesn't "check in" before implementing a new policy like, "All presentations must now be followed by a panic attack, because of that one time in 7th grade when you forgot your lines in the school play."

Nope. It just flips the switch and moves on.

And because these decisions are made far below our conscious awareness, we're left wondering, "Why does my chest tighten every time I speak in meetings?"

Hypnosis unravels these ancient, protective booby traps.

What's important to understand here is that none of this means your subconscious is broken. In fact, it's quite the opposite. It's doing its job too well. Like a smoke alarm that goes off every time you make toast.

The Unconscious **Authority**

And now that you've had a peek behind the curtain—seeing how the Unconscious Authority works, what kinds of weird emotional logic it follows, and how these patterns can create very real, very frustrating challenges—it's time for something new.

A fresh direction… one where you, the conscious adult, can team up with the subconscious and gently re-educate it on what's safe, what's true, and what can be finally released.

Are you ready to rewrite the outdated programming?

Ready to retire the over-zealous security guard and promote someone with a little more nuance?

Perfect. Let's get to work… You're about to reclaim authority—and logic—where it matters most!

Once you clear that mind clutter out, the doorways to what you desire are open.

Stephen Richards

JOE'S NOTE ON: NEGATIVE FOCUS

Focus too long on what's wrong, and you'll miss everything that's right.

What we focus on tends to expand in our perceptions. When we focus on problems, setbacks and imperfections in our lives, careers, or relationships, we are often so absorbed by what's "going wrong" that we miss what's going well!

The more we dwell on the negative, the more our mindset gets conditioned to expect (and therefore attract) more of the same.

In relationships, this might look like fixating on your partner's quirks or occasional mistakes, while forgetting the laughter or support they consistently offer.

At work, it might mean stressing over that one failed project and ignoring the five that went fabulous.

We must rebalance our perspective. Now this doesn't mean we should ignore problems, but rather to avoid letting them blind us to the good that's happening!

Practicing Gratitude and perspective aren't just "feel-good" exercises, they're powerful tools for staying grounded, hopeful, and resilient. Life isn't perfect, but neither is it all bad... that is, unless you convince yourself it is!

CHAPTER SIX
30 Days to the New and Improved You!

Before we dive in, I have to throw out a quick caution: *If you haven't read the previous chapters, stop right here. Go back.* Trust me on this.

Trying to implement what I'm about to share without understanding how your mind works is like showing up to build a house with only a hammer and no blueprints. You might make a little noise, but you're not going to assemble a safe and functional shelter.

Okay, now that we've got that out of the way...

You're probably thinking, "Alright, Joe... this is all fascinating, but what do I actually do to change my life?"

We've got to reprogram your subconscious mind. Specifically, we need to work with its ever-vigilant bouncer, the Unconscious Authority.

You've already learned that in order to create real, lasting change, your suggestions—your new desires, goals, beliefs—must make it past *The Critical Faculty*, that mental gatekeeper who's highly skeptical of anything new and prefers the cozy familiarity of the old.

Joe **Hammer**

Once we bypass that internal security guard, our suggestions can reach the subconscious mind, where the UA lives. This is the part of you that drives 95% of your daily behavior—usually without checking in with you first.

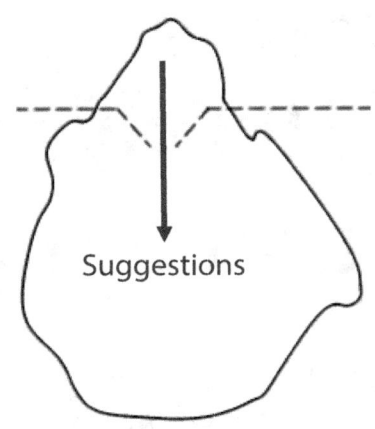

Now, as you've read, one way to get past that gatekeeper is through regressive hypnosis, which is a powerful and effective method. But let's be honest, most people don't have a reputable regression hypnotherapist living next door. That known, we're going to need a more accessible route.

The good news is that I've got one for you!

You might recall that your subconscious becomes most receptive when your conscious mind is relaxed. That's why your best ideas often show up when you're walking the dog, shampooing your hair, or zoning out during a long drive.

It's not magic, it's science. When you're doing something mundane, your conscious mind is busy handling the task, which allows your subconscious to stretch out, breathe, and play a little.

And that, my friend, is the first rule of "self" hypnosis... suggestions slip in when the conscious mind chills out.

And the best time of day for that to happen?

Right before you fall asleep.

The Unconscious **Authority**

Your conscious mind has clocked out for the day, and your body is begging for rest. But guess who's still working the night shift?

That's right, your Unconscious Authority and its managing of the subconscious mind.

While you snooze, your subconscious is busy keeping your body temperature regulated, your heart pumping, and your lungs doing their thing. It's basically the best employee you've got. And, during those final few minutes before you fall asleep—what we'll call the "twilight zone" of awareness. Your AU is wide open to suggestion.

I call it *The Golden Time of Bedtime Reprogramming*

You're about to discover that the very last thought, image, or idea you hold in your mind as you fall asleep will be repeated in your subconscious all night long.

Let me say it again...

The very last thought, image, or idea you hold in your mind as you fall asleep will be repeated in your subconscious all night long.

Kind of makes you want to stop falling asleep thinking about emails or unpaid bills, right? Instead, we're going to use this powerful window to send clear, focused suggestions directly to your Unconscious Authority—planting the seeds for real, lasting change.

You've got the tools. You've got the access point. You've got a highly suggestible subconscious just waiting for some updated instructions. And now, we're going to put it all into practice.

Let's look at exactly how this works—step by step.

The Wake Up Call

Let me walk you through a scenario you've almost certainly lived through...

You've got a fabulous vacation planned. Sun, sand, adventure... or maybe just a hotel that's not your house. Everything's packed. You've triple-checked your suitcase, your passport is where it should be, and you've set your alarm for 4:00 am because your flight leaves at 6:00.

You hit the pillow thinking, "I absolutely have to be up at 4:00 am."

You're exhausted—but of course, you can't sleep. Your brain is suddenly hosting a late-night logistics committee...

Did I pack my toothbrush?

Where are my car keys?

Is there gas in the car?

Did I print the boarding pass?

Did I call the post office to hold my mail?

You're mentally checking off every travel detail like a sleep-deprived TSA agent. And the more you think, the more your mind revs up. Sleep becomes an elusive goal.

Eventually, by some miracle, you finally drift off to sleep...

The Unconscious **Authority**

Then BAM, your eyes fly open at exactly 4:00 am.

And that alarm clock? Still silent.

So, what gives? How did you manage to wake up on time without so much as a "ding"?

Simple... *your subconscious was on the job.*

You went to bed with that wake-up time stamped into your brain like it was a matter of national security. On top of that, you fed your subconscious mind all the juicy supporting details... where you're going, what time the flight is, what could go wrong, and how crucial it is that you don't oversleep.

This cocktail of urgency and repetition told your subconscious, "Hey, this is important. Do not mess this up."

So it didn't.

Your subconscious took that message, filed it under "Urgency," and played it on loop all night long—until finally, it nudged you awake, on time, without any external help.

And that, dear reader, is the power of a clearly stated intent paired with emotional charge. It's also proof that your subconscious isn't just some background player. When it's given clear direction, it shows up like a trusted assistant determined to keep you on schedule.

And in case you're wondering, yes, this works outside of vacations too.

Now let's look at a real-life example from my own experience that shows just how reliable your UA can be when given the right marching orders.

The Neighborhood Bobcat

Let me tell you about one night when my subconscious decided to prove it's always paying attention—even when I'm not.

It was around 11:00 pm, and I was just about to drift off to sleep—right in that cozy, half-conscious zone where the pillow feels like heaven. Suddenly, ring ring... a phone call.

Slightly startled, I reached for my phone. It was from my neighbor, warning me that a bobcat had been spotted in the neighborhood.

Now, if you're not from Arizona, this might sound like an episode of National Geographic, Suburban Edition. But here, bobcats occasionally wander into developed communities in search of food, water, or maybe just a change of scenery. My neighbor, being thoughtful and aware that I have two bite-sized Chihuahuas, wanted to give me a heads-up—because to a hungry bobcat, my dogs probably look like a spicy two-for-one combo.

I thanked her, made a mental note to accompany the pups outside in the morning, and promptly fell asleep.

Fast forward to 3:00 am...

CRASH!

Some loud noise jolted me awake. No hesitation. No sleepy confusion. My first thought wasn't, "What was that?" Instead it

The Unconscious **Authority**

was, "The bobcat! It's in my backyard! It probably knocked over a chair, or the umbrella, or maybe it's doing laps in the pool!"

My adrenaline kicked in like I was on a wildlife rescue mission. I grabbed a flashlight and burst outside in my Spiderman onesie (not really), ready to face the feline intruder.

However...

There was no bobcat. Not even a housecat.

Turns out it was just a minor fender bender up the street. A car had lightly bumped into another, and the sound echoed just enough to wake me. No claws, no growls, no Chihuahuas in peril.

But here's the point... I didn't wake up thinking, Hmmm, what was that noise? My brain skipped right past logic and into bobcat battle mode. Why? Because I had planted that idea before drifting off to sleep.

My subconscious took the bobcat warning, highlighted it, underlined it and filed it under "Urgent Night Shift Information." And it kept looping the message all night, waiting for the slightest excuse to spring into action.

This is how the Unconscious Authority works. It doesn't reason, it reacts based on the emotional significance of the thoughts you feed it. And the last thing on your mind before you fall asleep is prime programming time.

I'm sure you've had moments like this too—where you woke up with a sudden solution, a clear direction, or an oddly specific dream about that thing you were pondering before bed.

Joe **Hammer**

That's why we've all heard the age-old advice, "Sleep on it."

Turns out, it's not just poetic wisdom. It's neuroscience in pajamas!

Bad Bedtime Rituals

One of the most common things clients come to me about? Sleepless nights, stress, and waking up feeling like they wrestled a bear in their dreams. So naturally, I ask a simple question:

"What do you watch before bed?"

And like clockwork, the answers roll in: *Dateline, CSI*, the 11 o'clock news… "Sometimes I just fall asleep with the TV on."

Yikes. No wonder you're dreaming about being chased through a thunderstorm by a guy in a ski mask.

When you're drifting off to sleep while someone's being interrogated for a triple homicide, your subconscious mind—that wonderful, unfiltered gatekeeper we've been talking about—takes it all in. And unlike your conscious mind, it doesn't stop to say, "Oh, this is just TV. That's not really a body in the trunk."

Nope. It processes everything as if it's actually happening… to you.

So while you're off in dreamland, the Unconscious Authority is saying, "Okay, there's clearly a crime spree happening. Better stay alert. No deep, restful sleep for you… we're on neighborhood watch tonight!"

The result? Your body thinks it's been surviving a war zone all

The Unconscious **Authority**

night. You wake up exhausted and sometimes anxious.

Now that you understand how powerful those pre-sleep moments are, how your subconscious clings to the last thing it heard or saw, it makes sense to be a little more intentional, doesn't it?

Save the true crime binge for daylight hours.

Instead of feeding it mayhem and melodrama, why not use that time to focus on the life you actually want?

Let's talk about how to turn this "quiet time" into a nightly opportunity to rewire your mind and create some real, positive change.

Wake Up to Change

Now that you know how to program your highly skilled—if a bit overprotective—internal guidance system, it's time to chart a simple, effective path for change. Don't worry, no hiking boots will be required.

Remember that first exercise in the book? The one where you listed the changes you want to make in your life? You did do that, right? If not, now's your chance to avoid the guilt and sneak back to it.

This time, we're taking it to the next level. We're going to supercharge those goals with vivid imagery, rich emotion, and sensory detail. Why? Because your subconscious speaks the language of feelings, images, and repetition—not logic and bullet points.

Let's say your original goal was, "I want to stop eating junk food."

Joe **Hammer**

Nice start. But it's time to reframe that vague, self-scolding goal into something your subconscious can sink its teeth into (pun intended).

Try something like, "I eat wholesome, nutritious foods and love how energized I feel! I adore fresh fruits and colorful veggies. I look forward to creating healthy meals."

Now let's kick things up a notch by engaging all five senses. This makes your subconscious feel like it's already living that change. And when it believes that? Boom. New habits start forming.

How It Looks

Close your eyes and imagine the change. What does success look like?

"I catch a glimpse of myself in the mirror and love what I see! I look slimmer, more confident, and my smile is practically high-definition. I shop for food with intention, reading labels like a nutrition-savvy detective. I walk taller, glow brighter, and genuinely enjoy this healthy new version of me."

How It Sounds

What are people saying to you? What compliments are you overhearing?

"Everyone keeps saying how amazing I look! My coworker asked what I've been doing because I 'look so fresh.' Even my gym buddy noticed I'm glowing. And let's be honest—when Karen from HR compliments me, it means something."

How It Feels

How do you physically and emotionally feel now that this change is a reality?

"I wake up energized and actually want to start the day. I feel lighter—physically, mentally, emotionally. I breeze through the grocery store like a health guru. After yoga, I feel like I've been hugged by the universe. I'm proud, calm, and maybe even a little smug—but the good kind."

How It Tastes

Yes, taste is important—especially when we're talking about food.

"Fresh fruit tastes like candy from nature. Stir-fried veggies make my taste buds do a happy dance. I've discovered that healthy food doesn't have to be boring; it can actually be delicious?!"

How It Smells

Aromas are powerful memory triggers, so why not use them to anchor your new lifestyle?

"The smell of garlic and herbs in my kitchen makes me feel like I'm on a cooking show. Every time I open my fridge and smell fresh produce, I feel like I'm investing in my future self."

Just like how your subconscious helped you wake up at 4:00 am for that big trip, it will respond to the detailed, emotional story you feed it. The clearer, richer, and more emotionally charged your vision is, the faster it becomes your reality.

So go ahead—build that benefit-loaded, emotionally vibrant mental movie of your desired change. The Unconscious Authority loves imagination. It's like candy for your programming system... but without the sugar crash.

And a quick tip... focus on one major change at a time. Your subconscious does best with clarity. Trying to overhaul your whole life in one go is like trying to train a puppy to sit, roll over and fetch all at once. Start with the most important goal, pack it full of sensory goodness, and go from there.

Now grab that goal, paint it with passion, and let's build the new you—one vibrant, subconscious-friendly night at a time.

Ready? Let's do this.

Launch Your Subconscious Motivation Process!

Alright, it's go time... time to put your brain to work while you sleep!

You've done the groundwork, you've dreamed the dreams, and now you're ready to hand off the night shift to your subconscious. While you sleep, your UA is going to quietly start putting your goals into motion, like a cosmic intern who never takes breaks.

The Unconscious **Authority**

But to get the UA properly on task, you need to give it clear instructions. Not vague mumbling like, "Ugh, I wish things were better." We're talking crystal-clear, emotionally charged, sensory-rich direction. Think of it as writing a letter to the universe with bold and specific bullet points.

This isn't some bedtime speech you need to recite out loud like a spell. Think of it more like a "journal of direction" a short, potent list of action words, positive outcomes, and vivid snapshots of the change you want to see in your life.

How does it work? Remember, your subconscious doesn't know the difference between real-life and vividly imagined life. You could be in sweatpants eating cereal for dinner, but if you visualize yourself crushing goals with energy, joy, and six-pack abs, your UA starts laying the groundwork for that reality.

So go all in—paint a Technicolor picture of the "new you." Describe how you look, feel, think, walk, eat, sleep, smell (yes, smell!) in this new version of yourself. Give your subconscious a full script to work from.

The Subconscious Motivation Worksheets

Now it's time to gather the emotional rocket fuel you created earlier and plug it into your Subconscious Motivation Worksheets. These worksheets are your official "order forms" to the subconscious.

Joe **Hammer**

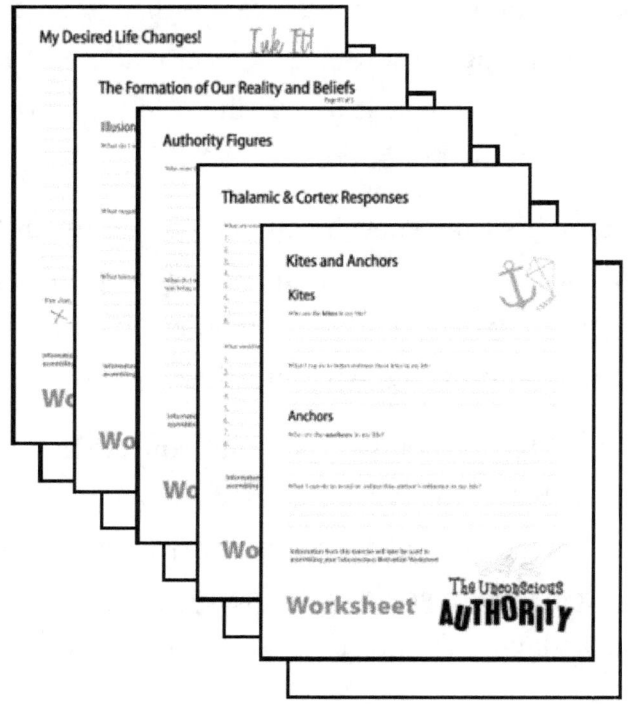

You can download full-size printable versions at www.UnconsciousAuthority.com/forms

Take all those juicy, specific words, images, and feelings from the earlier exercises and start transferring them here. These are the highlights you want your subconscious marinating in all night long.

You'll want to reference the following exercises:

- Your Desired Life Changes

- Your Empowered, Sensory-Driven Statements

The Unconscious **Authority**

- Visualizations of How It Looks, Sounds, Feels, Tastes, and Smells
- The Positive Opposites of Your Old Thought Patterns

Think of this as giving your subconscious a GPS destination—and then making the ride so emotionally compelling that it floors the gas pedal while you're off in dreamland.

Once you've completed your worksheets, you'll have a custom-designed, personalized, subconscious motivation plan—your internal night crew will finally have clear direction.

Let's get that "nighttime directive" in motion and start making change the easiest way possible… while you sleep!

Your Subconscious Rocket Fuel

Welcome to the deep-dive exercises! This is where we take all that self-reflection, dig it up, dust it off, and turn it into power for your subconscious motivation engine. Each exercise below plays a critical role in shaping your "nighttime directive"—that message you're planting for your Unconscious Authority to act on while you catch some Zzzs.

Ready? Let's make your inner world a lot more productive while your outer body is drooling on the pillow.

Motivation Worksheet #1: Your List of Desired Changes

Start by picking the single most important change you want in your life. Just one. We know, you probably have a whole

"Greatest Hits" album of improvements you'd love to make, but your UA works best when it's focused like a dog staring at a bacon strip.

For Example, "I want to be calmer and more patient with people" should come before, "I want to finally use that gym membership I've been paying for since 2019."

You can always revisit the other changes later, one at a time. Think sniper rifle, not a confetti cannon.

Motivation Worksheet #2: Illusions, Perceptions & Beliefs

Time to dig into the stuff you used to believe. What old stories or mental programming are still hanging around like expired condiments in your fridge?

Think back. What beliefs were handed down to you? These are usually with good intentions, but not-so-great outcomes.

How do they conflict with the change you now want? And how do you flip them?

For example, as it relates to the old saying, "money doesn't grow on trees."

"I live in an abundant universe. I earn money by helping others, and it flows easily into my life."

Boom. Belief flipped. Power restored.

Motivation Worksheet #3: Authority Figures

We've all had people in our past who "meant well" but left us

The Unconscious **Authority**

with... let's call them, "less-than-helpful mental souvenirs."

Ask yourself, "Who gave me those limiting directions or labels?"

What did they say or do that stuck with you?

How can you reinterpret their words into something that serves you now?

For example, relating to my high school assistant principal's remark about 'stop doodling and focus on the books.'

My reframe was, "He just didn't understand creativity as a career. But doodling is part of my ticket to success."

Sometimes the best revenge is rewriting the script!

Motivation Worksheet #4: Thalamic vs. Cortex Responses

Welcome to Brain Stuff 101.

Your Thalamic Response is your knee-jerk reaction—the button-push moment. The Cortex Response is your upgraded, rational, graceful comeback.

What situations still trigger you?

What would you prefer to feel or do instead?

Can you vividly imagine yourself responding in that better way?

Reframe "I get defensive when someone critiques me" to, "I now respond with curiosity and confidence, like a Zen master who is present and confident."

Motivation Worksheet #5: Kites and Anchors

Who are the people in your life who lift you up? (The kites). Who brings the storm clouds? (The anchors)

How can you spend more time with the lifters and less emotional energy on the drainers?

You can change your response to the anchors so their negativity doesn't land as deeply.

For example, "My coworker constantly complains" can be changed to, "I respond with empathy but don't absorb their energy. I carry peace like a shield and maybe with some noise-canceling earbuds."

Now, bring it all together!

Take the golden nuggets from each of these exercises and transfer them into your Subconscious Motivation Worksheets—especially in the VAK sections (Visual, Auditory, and Kinesthetic). Fill in:

- What you see in the new version of you
- What you hear (including what others are saying about the new you!)
- What you feel—emotionally and physically

Add as much vivid detail as you can. Journal your insights, your "aha" moments, and your boldest vision of the new you. The more you give your UA to work with, the more powerful the shift.

The Unconscious **Authority**

Ready to meet the upgraded you? Let's start wiring that transformation in tonight. And there's no Superman cape required—just a pen, some truth, and a cozy pillow!

Let the UA Take It From Here

Now that you've documented, detailed, and internalized the change you desire, it's time to pass the baton to the Unconscious Authority and let it do what it does best, silently guide you toward your chosen outcome while you snooze.

This isn't just a sleepy-time checklist of things to say before bed. No, this is a full-on sensory experience, a visual, auditory, and emotional preview of the new state of mind you're stepping into.

As you lie in bed and prepare to drift off, review your Subconscious Motivation Worksheets. Let the sights, sounds, and feelings you've written down swirl through your mind. Picture yourself already living that change. See it, feel it, hear it, maybe even smell or taste it. Be vivid! The UA loves vivid!

You've probably heard it takes 30 days to "break" a habit, right? Well, it's true. Sometimes longer. Most people give up, relying solely on willpower. That's like bringing a butter knife to a sword fight. It's not only the wrong tool, but it's highly ineffective.

The Subconscious Motivation Worksheets give you an edge. They take the pressure off the conscious mind by handing the job over to the UA, which thrives on emotionally-charged, sensory-rich instructions. All you need to do is glance over those phrases before bed, close your eyes, and let your imagination take the wheel.

If your mind starts to wander (and it probably will at first), gently steer it back. Keep applying those vivid details to the desired change—just like in the example of the 4:00 am wake-up for a big vacation. You didn't lie in bed thinking about your inbox or laundry that morning, did you? Instead you were laser-focused because you had something exciting waiting. That's the same energy you want here.

Stick with it. Do this for thirty consecutive evenings. If you miss a night, *start over*. Like anything new, it takes a little practice—but it will become a habit. And once it does, you'll have direct access to making lasting changes in your life.

Each night, review your Worksheets. No need to memorize anything, just soak in the sounds, feelings, and mental images of the "new you." Then, fall asleep while your UA works quietly in the background like your personal overnight success agent.

Avoid letting your mind drift to the random stuff of the day. Stay focused. Give your desired change the same energy and priority you would that early-morning flight. You've invested in this vision—treat it like it matters. Because it does.

In the morning when you wake up, offer a quick thank you to your UA for working while you rested. Then go about your day. If a positive thought about your change pops into your mind, pause and acknowledge it. That's your UA checking in.

Again, repeat this process each night for 30 days. You're not

The Unconscious **Authority**

just reinforcing the change, you're rewiring your mind with new programming. Many people continue this practice beyond thirty days, using it as a tool for refinement and deeper transformation. You can too.

Well, there you have it, the stealthy, behind-the-scenes process of reprogramming your Unconscious Authority to deliver the results you actually want! And no lab coat will be required.

You're now fully equipped to head off on your journey. I genuinely wish you the absolute best that life has to offer. And remember, just like Dorothy from The Wizard of Oz, the power has been within you all along. No ruby slippers necessary—just a little intention and consistency!

It's your turn now. Go get it. And may your Unconscious Authority become your most loyal (and quietly brilliant) co-pilot in life.

Wishing you clarity, joy, and just the right amount of magic!

Success is the sum of small efforts, repeated day-in and day-out
Robert Collier

JOE'S NOTE ON: ASSUMPTIONS

The mind doesn't always report the truth; it many times writes fiction and calls it fact.

Assumptions can be a common trap in both relationships and professional business settings. We often mistake our untested beliefs or gut feelings for reliable information. An assumption might feel like a solid conclusion, but without real evidence, it's just a guess. Assumptions become the fodder or data your brain uses to create a story.

When we build decisions, plans, or reactions around those guesses—especially in high-stakes situations like business or personal conflict—we're treating shaky information as though it's fact. This is where the trouble often begins.

Assumptions can many times look strategic or intelligent on the surface. They often appear to be based on logic, confidence, or intuition. But underneath, they haven't been verified.

In business, this could mean launching a product based on what you think customers want rather than what market research has provided.

Strategies built on assumptions is like building a house on a faulty foundation. Real strategy is rooted in tested truths—not assumptive shortcuts.

Assumptions in business and relationships can quietly sabotage progress by treating imaginative truths as fact.

ADDENDUM
Hypnosis Myths and Misconceptions

Most people plod along day after day, experiencing only a small percentage of their life's full potential. They often hope that luck or some other "mysterious power" will magically turn things around. What they don't realize is that a divine power to create change is already within them—just waiting to be called into action like a loyal employee that's been quietly standing by asking, "You ready yet?"

A far-fetched idea?

Not at all. It's a scientifically supported truth. The secret starts with self-awareness. Hypnosis is simply a self-awareness expansion technique. It helps you override the outdated programming of your past and puts you on the path toward health, happiness, and the kind of success that doesn't require lottery tickets or midnight manifesting rituals.

Below are some of the most common questions I get about hypnosis and hypnotherapy—along with a few of the biggest myths that still linger.

Joe **Hammer**

What is hypnosis?

Let's clear this up right away... hypnosis is nothing like what you've seen in movies or cartoons. There's no swinging watch, spooky voice, or mind-controlling wizard in a cape. Sorry to disappoint you drama lovers out there...

This is not hypnosis!

In reality, hypnosis is a natural, relaxed state of focused awareness. You enter it all the time without even trying. Ever daydream while showering, mowing the lawn, walking the dog, or eating cereal while staring into space? Congratulations, you've been lightly hypnotized.

These "automatic" activities are stored in the subconscious. While you're coasting in routine mode, your mind naturally shifts to a different level of consciousness. It's a light trance—nothing magical, nothing mystical. Just your mind doing what it was designed to do, operate efficiently and creatively when your conscious guard is down.

Daydreaming is actually the first level of a trance state. Hypnosis isn't sleep, and it's not unconsciousness. During hypnosis, your body and conscious mind are relaxed while your subconscious becomes highly attentive and open to suggestion—suggestions you choose. It's not mind control. *It's mind cooperation.*

Why do some people have doubts about hypnosis?

Hollywood and pop culture have done a phenomenal job of completely misrepresenting hypnosis.

For centuries, hypnosis was lumped in with spiritualism, witchcraft, and other misunderstood phenomena. Toss in a few spooky B-movies, dramatic stage acts, and TV shows with over-the-top hypnotists, and voilà... a full-blown misconception that hypnosis is either a creepy carnival trick or a shady form of mind control.

The truth? Hypnosis is a clinical, evidence-based practice. In fact, the American Medical Association recognized it as a legitimate therapeutic tool back in 1958. That's right, your subconscious got an official thumbs-up from the medical community over 60 years ago.

Are the results of hypnosis permanent?

The honest answer is... *it depends*. Yeah, I know, not the most satisfying response—but stay with me.

For some, hypnotic suggestions stick like glue. For others, they need occasional reinforcement, especially if they've spent years repeating a behavior. But the good news is that hypnosis is cumulative. The more you practice, the stronger and more permanent the changes become.

And just like brushing your teeth, self-hypnosis is most effective when it becomes part of your regular routine. You're not trying to fix everything overnight. You're laying down new neural tracks in the subconscious that will carry you forward with less resistance and a lot less drama during the process.

What does hypnosis feel like?

This is a common question for many folks. Some people think they'll be swept into some altered, cosmic state where they float above their body or lose total awareness like they're under anesthesia. Others expect fireworks or a mystical fog to roll in. Sorry, but it's not that dramatic... and that's a good thing.

Hypnosis feels like a deep state of calm. It's similar to that relaxed twilight moment when you're about to fall asleep, but still aware enough to hear your dog snoring. You may even wonder, "Am I doing this right?" which is a great sign. It means you're still aware, just relaxed.

You're not unconscious. You can open your eyes at any time. You remember what was said. And—let's address the classic myth—you won't bark like a dog or cluck like a chicken... unless you really want to.

During a session, your attention may wander. Thoughts will drift in and out. That's completely normal. In fact, it's proof that you're not "asleep." Hypnosis is not about losing control, it's about shifting focus inward and engaging your imagination to create new possibilities.

The Unconscious **Authority**

Does hypnosis weaken the will?

Quite the opposite. Hypnosis strengthens your will. It works with your will—not against it—by bypassing the critical filter of your conscious mind and helping you align your subconscious with what you actually desire. It's like giving your internal GPS a clearer destination—one that your conscious and subconscious agree on for once.

Far from weakening your will, hypnosis empowers it by removing the mental clutter and unhelpful beliefs.

What is the subconscious mind?

The conscious mind is the part you think with. It's the analytical, logical voice that asks for evidence, makes lists, and sometimes overthinks everything.

The subconscious mind, on the other hand, is where your habits, beliefs, memories, and emotional responses live. It's where the "autopilot" lives. Most of that programming was installed before you were old enough to question it. That means you're often reacting to life based on old, unexamined beliefs from childhood, some of which were planted with good intentions, but may now be running the show in unhelpful ways.

Hypnosis helps you access that deeper layer and update the old code. You're not deleting anything, you're just installing better, more current software that's aligned with who you are today and where you want to go.

Joe **Hammer**

How does the subconscious accept hypnotic suggestions?

The subconscious mind is not the part of you that analyzes, debates, or second-guesses. That's the conscious mind's job—and it's very good at it.

Hypnotic suggestions work by bypassing the conscious, critical, overthinking gatekeeper. Once a suggestion makes it through, if it aligns with your personal values and beliefs, the subconscious tends to accept it literally, as a new operating instruction. It's like rewriting the software while the computer's still running. No reboot needed!

But don't worry, your subconscious isn't gullible. If a suggestion contradicts your ethics or common sense, it's booted out like a bad tenant. That's why hypnosis isn't about mind control. It's about focused reprogramming... *with your consent.*

Who can be hypnotized?

If you have an average intelligence, the ability to focus, and a semi-open mind (and you're not trying to prove it won't work), you can be hypnotized. You don't need to be "suggestible." You just need to participate.

Now, is it more challenging for some people? Sometimes, yes. Not because they're "bad subjects," but because of underlying resistance. This can come from a fear of losing control, a misunderstanding of what hypnosis feels like, or even good ol' fashioned nerves. Some folks just aren't used to relaxing!

The key is identifying why the resistance is there. Once it's understood, it can be cleared, and then hypnosis becomes accessible.

How does hypnosis help people?

In simple terms, hypnosis helps people change from the inside out.

It's like giving your subconscious a personal development seminar—minus the overpriced tickets and the loud music. Hypnosis helps rewire emotional patterns, beliefs, habits, and even long-buried potential. Instead of dragging your past like an overpacked suitcase, you get to travel lighter.

Let's face it, your conscious mind is great at solving math problems and choosing what to wear. But when it comes to deep emotional issues, it doesn't hold much influence. Hypnosis steps in where conscious willpower taps out, helping you shift beliefs and responses that have been stuck for decades.

It's not magic. It's just the most efficient way to update the inner programming that's been secretly running the show!

How long has hypnosis been around?

From ancient rituals to tribal ceremonies, to the temples of ancient Egypt, forms of trance and suggestion have been used throughout human history. It's only the clinical applications that are "new." Hypnosis has evolved, modernized, and now has comfy chairs and ambient music.

So no, this isn't a trend. It's a time-tested, brain-based tool with a history longer than most belief systems.

Joe **Hammer**

Will I be able to go into the hypnotic state?

Yes. You already have... many, many times.

Ever been so into a movie that someone spoke to you and you didn't hear them? Or gotten lost in a book to the point that hours passed in what felt like minutes? That's the same brain-wave pattern hypnosis taps into.

In hypnosis, your focus shifts inward. Your body relaxes, your mind becomes more open, and the outside world fades into the background. You're not out of control, you're just deeply, pleasantly focused.

So if you're worried about whether you can "go under," relax. You've already been under, you just didn't realize it had a name!

Can I become "stuck" in hypnosis or not "wake up?"

Absolutely not. Hypnosis isn't sleep. It just feels wonderfully relaxing like that sweet spot between awake and dreaming. You're always in control and aware on some level. You could open your eyes and walk away at any time (but most people don't want to, because it feels so good!)

You don't need to "wake up" because you never fell asleep. You just shifted your attention inward. That's all. No disappearing acts or scary sci-fi scenarios, I promise!

The Unconscious **Authority**

Can a person be hypnotized against their will?

No, not happening. Hypnosis is a voluntary state. It requires consent, participation, and at least a little bit of curiosity. You cannot be hypnotized unless you want to be. And even then, you must allow it to happen.

A hypnotist can't "do it to you." They simply guide you. You create the experience. It's a bit like following the directions on a GPS; you still have to steer the car.

And let's bust the big myth... nobody can make you cluck like a chicken or rob a bank unless you were already planning to do that. You always retain your personal boundaries, values, and ability to say, "Nope, not doing that!"

Will I divulge secrets or always tell the truth?

This is another myth from the movies. Hypnosis is not a truth serum. You're not hooked up to a lie detector, and you're not going to start blurting out your high school locker combination or deepest secrets unless you choose to.

You're fully aware during hypnosis. You won't say anything you wouldn't say while awake. That said, sometimes old memories resurface... things you hadn't consciously recalled in years. And while that can be surprising, it's often exactly what helps people unlock and resolve deep issues.

So no, you won't "spill the beans" unless you want to share something that helps you heal, move forward, or better understand yourself.

Will my problems go away if the hypnotist tells me so?

Oh, if only it were that easy!

Truth is, hypnosis is a powerful tool, but it's still a tool. It doesn't do the work for you. Think of the hypnotist as a guide.

Hypnosis helps you access the inner control room of your subconscious. But you've still got to sit in the driver's seat. Hypnosis allows you to reframe, rewire, and reinforce positive behavior, but you're an active partner in the process.

So no, the hypnotist doesn't just snap their fingers and poof, your problems disappear. But together, you can create real, lasting change. Team effort, Grasshopper. Team effort.

Can hypnosis turn me into a different person?

No! Hypnosis doesn't give you a personality transplant.

You'll still be you; you'll just be a freer, lighter, maybe more confident version of yourself. Kind of like the "you" you always knew you could be, minus the self-doubt or fear that's been squatting in your mental space.

Now, can your behavior change? Absolutely. Let's say you overcome chronic anxiety or stop procrastinating or finally tell your

The Unconscious **Authority**

inner critic to take a long walk. That might look like a personality shift to others, but you're not changing who you are, you're just peeling off layers that weren't serving you.

On repeated occasions will I go into hypnosis easier?

Yes! Like any skill, the more you do it, the easier it gets.

The first time, your mind might be saying, "Wait, what are we doing here?" But over time, your subconscious says, "Oh, this again—I know the drill." You begin to relax more quickly and drop into that focused state with ease.

It's like going to the gym. At first, your muscles complain. Later, they just show up and ready for the workout!

Is it possible to hypnotize myself?

Yes! And once you learn how, it's like having your own private mindset coach on call 24/7.

Self-hypnosis is simply you guiding yourself into that same relaxed, focused state. Using suggestion, visualization, and affirmations, you can direct your subconscious. It's incredibly useful for managing stress, motivation, performance, and just about anything else you can think of.

Most people can learn self-hypnosis with a little guidance and practice. It's a life skill you'll wonder how you ever lived without!

Joe **Hammer**

So what all can I do with hypnosis?

Here's where it gets fun, because the possibilities are vast.

Hypnosis is especially effective for changing habit patterns—those deeply rooted behaviors that keep tripping us up. Whether it's biting your nails, smoking, avoiding public speaking, or feeling overwhelmed in social situations, hypnosis can help you shift those patterns at their core.

But let's get something straight... hypnosis isn't a way to skip out on personal responsibility. It doesn't replace willpower, it enhances it. It doesn't take away the need for effort, it just removes the resistance that makes the effort feel like a mountain.

If you're truly ready to change, hypnosis is the lever that helps lift the old story off your back. It gives you momentum. It gets your inner voice saying, "Yes, we can," instead of "Here we go again..."

The easier you can make it inside your head, the easier it will make things outside your head.
Richard Bandler

Here's a list of just some of the areas where people have experienced powerful breakthroughs through hypnosis:

Confidence	Panic attacks
Health	Sports enhancement
Addictions	Motivation
Stress management	Public speaking
Weight management	Emotional trauma
Anger control	Pain management
Creativity	Phobias
Relaxation	Sleep issues
Self-confidence	Self-esteem
Memory improvement	Concentration
Study skills	Test anxiety
Feelings of sadness	Low energy

Attention or hyperactivity challenges

Unwanted habits and behaviors

And more!

It's not about whether hypnosis can help... it's about whether you're ready to make a shift in your life. So, let me ask you this, *which ones are you ready to tackle?*

GET JOE'S OTHER BOOKS!...

BLANK TO BRILLIANT

Develop the Ultimate Soft Skill in Effective Business Communications!

Transform the way you communicate! Say goodbye to dull conversations and hello to a whole new level of engagement and productivity! Discover the surprising power of improv and how it can transform the way you communicate, helping you to build stronger relationships, foster creativity, and navigate any challenge with confidence!

www.BlankToBrilliantBook.com

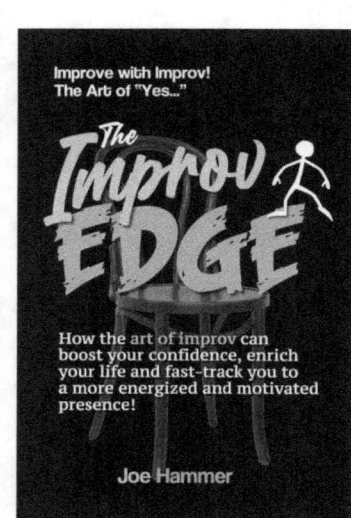

THE IMPROV EDGE

How the art of improv can boost your confidence, enrich your life and fast-track you to a more energized and motivated presence!

The Improv Edge will introduce you to essential improv skills that will assist you in creativity, spontaneity, listening, acceptance, confidence building, collaborative creativity and teamwork ... and all in an active and fun way! Now you can quickly undo rigid thinking, improve your social skills and boost your self-confidence!

www.TheImprovEdgeBook.com

MEET THE AUTHOR

Joe Hammer's fascination with the human mind began early. As a teenager, he became driven by a single, compelling question: *Why do some people achieve extraordinary success and wealth, while others—equally smart and capable—struggle to get by?* That burning curiosity set him on a lifelong quest to understand the hidden forces that shape behavior, success, and human potential.

The turning point came in the most unexpected of places—a comedy club. Working a second job as a comedy stage magician, Joe found himself opening for a hypnotist. But it wasn't the audience that was hypnotized—it was *him*. Mesmerized by what he saw onstage, he was struck by the power of suggestion and the untapped potential within the subconscious mind.

That moment sparked an intense personal journey. Joe immersed himself in the study of hypnosis, eventually transitioning his act into a hypnosis-based stage show. But entertainment was only the beginning. He soon dove deeper, pursuing professional training in clinical hypnotherapy. His studies led him to specialize in regression therapy—helping clients uncover and resolve pivotal childhood events that silently shaped their adult struggles, beliefs, and patterns.

As Joe's work evolved, he integrated additional transformative modalities, including Neuro-Linguistic Programming (NLP) and Timeline Therapy. Out of this blend of techniques, he developed **Rapid Changeworks**®, a multi-process model designed to uncover and reprogram the subconscious beliefs, emotional triggers, and internal narratives that keep people stuck.

In addition to his therapeutic work, Joe also helps business owners start and grow their ventures through one-on-one consulting and mentoring. He is also active in the world of improv, using spontaneous performance and communication training as a tool for personal and professional growth. Visit Joe at www.JoeHammer.com

Joe **Hammer**

Dear Joe,

I am sending you heart felt Thanks for my hypnosis session. Within the last 3 months I have noticed subtle changes in my way of Thinking & living.

My Self confidence & Self acceptance has increased. I am finding an excitement about my life that I have not really felt before.

Thank you for your compassion, caring and professionalism,

You Rock

Annie

The Unconscious **Authority**

SOME OF JOE'S ORIGINAL QUOTES...

The mind doesn't always report the truth; it many times writes fiction and calls it fact.

Focus too long on what's wrong and you'll miss everything that's right.

Sometimes it's witnessing another's darkness that allows you to awaken to your own light.

Cheerleaders can boost your spirit but they shouldn't call your plays.

The moment you choose to be real, everything false begins to fall away.

When we draw our paths into our present, we trap ourselves in battles that no longer exist.

Anger is the outward eruption of deep pain, fear, and frustration that lurks within us.

Your thoughts are reflection of your deepest historic beliefs of the past, shaping the reality you experience in the present.

There are many who will tell you what your ego wants to hear but those who truly care will speak from the heart, telling what you need to hear.

A wandering, spiraling mind focusing on the darkness can make us blind to the light that's present.

The past echoes in the present break old patterns. Choose intention over repetition.

Ego builds walls while burning bridges, leaving only the ashes of what could have been.

Visit Joe on Instagram@heyjoehammer for more!

www.ingramcontent.com/pod-product-compliance
Lightning Source LLC
Chambersburg PA
CBHW070556300426
44113CB00010B/1283